The
Astrology
of
2012
And How It Affects You

The
Astrology
of
2012
And How It Affects You

MARCUS MASON

HAY HOUSE

Australia • Canada • Hong Kong • India
South Africa • United Kingdom • United States

First published and distributed in the United Kingdom by:
Hay House UK Ltd, 292B Kensal Rd, London W10 5BE. Tel.: (44) 20 8962 1230;
Fax: (44) 20 8962 1239. www.hayhouse.co.uk

Published and distributed in the United States of America by:
Hay House, Inc., PO Box 5100, Carlsbad, CA 92018-5100. Tel.: (1) 760 431 7695 or (800) 654 5126;
Fax: (1) 760 431 6948 or (800) 650 5115. www.hayhouse.com

Published and distributed in Australia by:
Hay House Australia Ltd, 18/36 Ralph St, Alexandria NSW 2015. Tel.: (61) 2 9669 4299;
Fax: (61) 2 9669 4144. www.hayhouse.com.au

Published and distributed in the Republic of South Africa by:
Hay House SA (Pty), Ltd, PO Box 990, Witkoppen 2068. Tel./Fax: (27) 11 467 8904.
www.hayhouse.co.za

Published and distributed in India by:
Hay House Publishers India, Muskaan Complex, Plot No.3, B-2, Vasant Kunj, New Delhi –
110 070. Tel.: (91) 11 4176 1620; Fax: (91) 11 4176 1630. www.hayhouse.co.in

Distributed in Canada by:
Raincoast, 9050 Shaughnessy St, Vancouver, BC V6P 6E5. Tel.: (1) 604 323 7100;
Fax: (1) 604 323 2600

© Marcus Mason, 2011

A catalogue record for this book is available from the British Library.

ISBN 978-1-84850-498-1

Printed and bound in Great Britain by
TJ International, Padstow, Cornwall.

*This book is dedicated to my partner Sue,
in appreciation of her tireless, detailed and patient
editing, and for helping to keep my feet on the Earth,
while my mind was floating about in the Cosmos!*

*It is also dedicated to all those who take up
the challenge to live fully from their heart.*

'Humanity models itself on Earth
Earth models itself on Heaven
Heaven models itself on the Dao
The Dao models itself on what is natural'

Lao-Tzu, author of *Dao de Jing*
(translated by Peter Firebrace)

CONTENTS

Contents

COLOUR PLATES

ACKNOWLEDGEMENTS

I am indebted to all those who have been my teachers of astrology, planetary dynamics, and personal and planetary healing, and to all those who have, knowingly or unknowingly, enabled the writing and publication of this book:

Ron Buckle, William Buehler, Nicolya Christi, Michael Davies, Susanne Deuter, Claire de Valero, John P. Fletcher, John and Angie Hicks, Bruno and Louise Huber, Brett Kellett, Tracy Mack, Hamish Miller, Michael Mirdad, Jill Moore, Michelle Pilley and all the team at Hay House UK, Robin Rose, Pam Tyler, Professor J.R. Worsley, Caroline Wyndham; with deep gratitude to Master Djwhal Khul and Master Lin, for their inspiration.

Thanks and acknowledgment to the copyright holders for permission to quote from the following works: Peter Firebrace BAc MBAcC, for his translation of Chapter 25 of the *Dao de Jing*; Gary Renard *The Disappearance of the Universe*, Hay House, Inc.; Dane Rudhyar *An Astrological Mandala*, Random House Inc.; Joseph Campbell *The Masks of God, vol II: Oriental Mythology*, Penguin Arkana © 1962, reprinted by permission of the Joseph Campbell Foundation (jcf.org); Richard Tarnas *Cosmos and Psyche*, Plume.

Thanks too, for their inspiring writing, to Stephen Arroyo, Bernadette Brady, Paul Broadhurst, Barbara Hand Clow, Robert Coon, Ronnie Gale Dreyer, Demetra George, Liz Greene, Robin Heath, John Major Jenkins, John Michell, Alan Oken, Gary Renard, Dane Rudhyar, Martin Schulman, Richard Tarnas.

Astrology and Astronomy Charts, Images, and Colour Plates:

Astrology Charts and Maps created with Solar Fire Gold and Solar Maps v3, Esoteric Technologies Pty Ltd and Astrolabe Software.

Astronomical Star Charts produced by Chris Marriott's SkyMap Pro.

The inclusion of images from NASA, Hubble and ESA does not imply any endorsement by them of the views or opinions expressed in this book.

Thanks to Anthony Ayiomamitis for permission to use his photo 'Summer Milky Way (Sagittarius)'; www.perseus.gr.

Image of 'Ophiuchus and Serpens' (Chapter 4):
Taurus Poniatowski, Serpentarius from Urania's Mirror constellation cards, published *c.*1825, reproduced courtesy of OldBookArt.com; www.gallery.oldbookart.com.

INTRODUCTION

Another Book About 2012?

Whatever you believe about the nature and meaning of Life, there can be no doubt that we are living in 'interesting times'. Many centuries ago, the Maya of Central America[1] were aware of the significance of this time.

The Mayan 'Long Count' Calendar is derived from their understanding of vast cosmic time cycles. According to their calculations, one of these cycles, lasting for nearly 26,000 years, will end on 21 December 2012. The Maya clearly understood the cyclical nature of Time, and that as one cycle ends, so another begins.

In recent years, there has almost been an 'epidemic' of books, websites and even a Hollywood disaster movie about 2012. Many books have included detailed explorations of Mayan cosmology, from both orthodox and unorthodox perspectives, as well as several psychic or 'channelled' takes on what is happening. There is a wide variety of websites ranging from very literal interpretations of Mayan symbology to the sublimely inspirational, as well as the astronomically impossible. So why should there be any need for another book about 2012?

Much speculation and fear has been generated about the significance of the Mayan calendar 'end date'. Much of this speculation and practically *all* of the fear, however, stem from either incomplete or inaccurate understanding of what will actually occur in 2012. We are warned variously that there may be a magnetic pole reversal, or even that the Earth's crust may do a 'flip', or 'crustal displacement'; or that it heralds the return of planet Nibiru, which allegedly has a 3,600-year orbit around the Sun and Sirius. Already, several Internet videos claim to show planet Nibiru emerging from behind the Sun; this sensational-looking 'phenomenon' is actually produced by pointing a mobile phone camera directly at the Sun, creating a smaller, false image of the Sun next to it.

While none of these possibilities can be completely discounted, the key here is 'discernment'. With all the hype around 2012, it is important to engage your left and right brain together; this is one of the most important 'lessons' for everyone at this time. While we can be on shaky ground if we choose to listen only to the voice of reason, we are on equally shaky ground if we choose to throw reason out of the window and rely solely on intuition. Now is the time for the mind and heart to work together in harmony and mutual respect – that is the essence of the change that 2012 brings.

Throughout time, all genuine spiritual teachers have urged that we question and check the spiritual assertions of others; that we test or verify our own spiritual insights and realizations to see if they hold true in practice. Jesus, that great proponent of Faith, allowed Thomas to touch his wounds to prove that it was him, when he appeared to the disciples after the Crucifixion. The requirement for blind faith from the Christian Church came much later, as a means of control and the gradual elimination of spiritual discernment. This ultimately led to the loss of our direct personal connection with our God, or inner spiritual Self, so that 'spiritual truth' became something 'out there', with our access to it controlled by priests or scholars. Those who did maintain a direct awareness of the spiritual worlds were persecuted and sometimes mercilessly removed.

Now it appears that we have reached the other side of that particular coin and are in danger that 'truth' is moving more and more into the hands and control of materialist scientists, sceptics and atheists. Their particular version of 'truth', however, is not based on current science and the consciousness-expanding discoveries of those at the forefront of Quantum Physics. Instead it is in the hands of those who seek to reduce consciousness to a combination of the genetic coding in our DNA and the chemical excretions of the brain and other organs. If something can't be measured, verified, or 'proved' according to quite narrow criteria, then it is rejected.

Meanwhile those at the cutting edge of Quantum Physics are telling us that they cannot say for certain whether particles exist, and that matter probably does not really exist, all that exists is consciousness. At the cutting edge of cosmology, astronomers know that they cannot account for 80 per cent of the matter in the Universe – so-called 'dark matter'. There is a lot more uncertainty involved in the Universe than most are willing to acknowledge.

What *is* certain about 2012 is that even the Mayan Elders say that they do not know what will happen. As they are the current keepers of this lineage of ancient wisdom, perhaps it would be wise to listen to *them*. They seem quite bemused by the many Mayan experts and scholars, who are speculating about what will happen. What *is* known is that the Mayan Long Count Calendar reaches the end of one cycle on 21 December 2012 and then a new cycle starts. It seems that how the new cycle will manifest will be dependent upon our collective thoughts, attitudes, beliefs and behaviour, as we approach the end and afterward.

A particular facet of the post-Enlightenment[2] western mind is that it does not like uncertainty or paradox. Increasingly however, quantum physics is telling us that nothing is certain; that everything influences everything else, to the extent that atomic particles behave differently when they are being observed, to when they are not being observed. This means that the very fact that we are observing something changes its nature. In other words, we cannot separate ourselves from the rest of the Universe, in spite of our best efforts to do so.

Ancient cultures have always known that all life is connected. The delusion that we are somehow separate from the natural world is a peculiarity limited to the 'civilized Western mind' of recent centuries. Thankfully, science is now rediscovering the wisdom of old – that all is connected, and that everything affects everything else.

If the mere fact of our presence at an event can help to influence its outcome, then how much more so will our conscious thoughts, loving feelings or focused intentions influence the world around us. This is what Buddhism has referred to, for a very long time, as mindfulness. When we are mindful, we are fully present in the moment and fully aware of the influence that our thoughts, feelings and actions may have on others and on our environment.

This book was undertaken to give a balanced perspective on the Mayan Calendar end date, from the viewpoint of Western astrology; also, to help clarify what is actually happening astronomically, using simple language and understandable terminology.

I make no claim to be a Mayan 'scholar' or 'expert'; in fact the only people who can make that claim are current day Mayan Elders. Any Western investigator of Mayan mythology is inevitably at a disadvantage, because we are looking at this highly complex, intricate, ancient mythology from the outside; if we have not been brought up within the culture that has engendered, nurtured and sustained this rich mythology, then we lack a crucial perspective on the mythological archetypes that underpin it. The Mayan Calendar, however, does have a sound astronomical basis; this being the case, it is possible for us to explore it from the perspective of our own Western astrology, astronomy and mythology.

Soul-Purpose Astrology

'Soul-Purpose Astrology' is not concerned with predicting the outcome of events; it is more about exploring the underlying energetic patterns, and the psychological and spiritual tendencies that are inherent in any given moment. Looked at in this way, astrology can give clear indications of the best ways to approach certain life situations. It can help us to see what may be required for our inner learning, for adjusting our attitudes and resolving internal conflicts in order to embrace our full creative potentials.

After nearly 30 years of practising and teaching astrology, it is probably more accurate for me to describe this approach as 'Astro-Cosmology'. Astrology has gained, in some circles, a somewhat negative, sometimes fanciful, and certainly non-scientific reputation. The discoveries of Astronomy and Particle Physics, however, increasingly resemble the assertions and beliefs that Western astrology has evolved over the last few thousand years. As with all evolving systems of knowledge or belief, it is essential to keep pace with, and adapt to, the latest scientific discoveries.

The discoveries of the last few decades are confirming what many have intuitively known, namely that everything in the Cosmos is subtly interconnected and interdependent; from the effects of the gravitational interdependence of the planetary orbits, to the growing understanding of the effects of the Solar Wind on the magnetic fields of the Earth and other planets, to the awareness of the existence of 'dark matter'.

Each new discovery brings another 'aha' realization to the world of astrology, helping to make sense of this ancient wisdom, and why it has had such a profound hold on the human imagination for thousands of years. One of our greatest and most respected scientist-astronomers, Sir Isaac Newton, had an abiding interest in astrology; yet this is ignored or regarded as a mere 'aberration' by modern scientific materialists. The most pertinent rebuff to such scepticism came from Sir Isaac Newton himself; when challenged by Sir Edmond Halley about the validity of astrology, he replied, 'Sir, I have studied it, you have not'.

Like so many topics concerned with the more subtle, energetic realities of the Universe, or with inner psychological and spiritual processes, or with the workings of 'alternative' medicine (which has been around thousands of years longer than 'orthodox' medicine), those who criticize or condemn such things often have a very incomplete understanding of even the most basic principles.

The popular astrology of Sun-sign columns in the daily newspapers is an exceedingly simplified, watered-down version of a profound, complex and very ancient wisdom. This wisdom is firmly based in the astronomical movements, cycles and interactions between the Sun, Moon and all of the planets in relation to the 'background' of the constellations of the zodiac.

In this book, we will see that astrology is a profound and accurate means of understanding not only the rhythms and time cycles of the planets' orbits around the Sun, but also the much larger time cycles of our Solar System in relation to the Milky Way Galaxy.

When we begin to explore and study this vast subject from a balanced standpoint, freed from popular superstition and misconceptions, we may see why it has been embraced by such great scientific minds as Johannes Kepler and Sir Isaac Newton, or by pioneers of psychoanalysis and psychosynthesis, such as Carl Jung and Roberto Assagioli, or by deep thinkers and philosophers, such as Ptolemy and Aristotle.

These great thinkers were by no means feeble-minded or gullible, yet many scientists still choose to dismiss astrology as aberration, delusion or superstition. Perhaps this attitude tells us more about the limitations of those who are judging or criticizing, than it does about the wisdom of those who perceived that the movements of the planets have an influence upon our behaviour patterns.

Such considerations apply even more when we come to explore the astrological awareness of the Ancients, from the builders of the Pyramids and Stonehenge, to the cosmology and architectural achievements of the ancient Egyptians, to the Incas of South America and the Toltecs, Mayans and Aztecs of Central America. The Mayans, without the aid of computers, but using simple, detailed observations, were able to evolve highly complex and intricate calendars of vast cosmic time cycles, accurate to within hours; they then represented these cycles through the building of magnificent, mind-bogglingly accurate pyramids.

What we tend to forget, when we try to think about how this could be possible, is that in the days of Stonehenge, the Egyptian Pyramids, or the Pyramids of the Mayans and Aztecs, people lived under the stars, with no light pollution to obscure their stunning view of the night sky. There were no books to distract them, no TV, no computers, no telescopes even, just the awe-inspiring sense of observing and feeling the daily, monthly and yearly dance of the Earth and Moon on their journey through the vastness of space, evident for all to see, every night. Here were people who knew that their survival depended upon understanding and predicting the yearly cycles of the crops, the rising and setting of the Sun, or the yearly flooding of the Nile in Egypt. Over time, they were able to link these with the movements of the Sun, Moon and wandering planets that appeared to bring with them changes in their circumstances and fortunes.

When Professor Alexander Thom undertook his remarkably accurate surveys of the geometry of many of the stone circles of the British Isles in the 1950s and '60s, people marvelled at how the 'primitive' builders of these megaliths could have possibly understood the Pythagorean geometry that Thom found in the layout of many of the stone circles. This viewpoint typifies the 'blind spot' of our modern culture, which has been educated in ways that teach us to think from the theoretical level of the academic mind, and has become divorced from the realities of the natural world.

The builders of these stone circles and standing stones clearly learned their geometry by observing the movements of the Sun, Moon and stars in their yearly cycles, which they then marked, first with wooden posts and later with stone monuments. This was clearly a science, based on practical observations, from which they discovered and extrapolated the underlying mathematical and geometrical relationships of the cycles and patterns of the Sun, Moon, planets and Cosmos. These patterns and relationships are inherent in the nature of things; if we too can simply, accurately and open-mindedly observe the nature of things, then we will inevitably understand these underlying patterns and cycles.

The Mayan 'End Date' (December Solstice 2012)

The essential thing about the December Solstice in 2012 is that it marks a turning point in a vast Galactic time cycle; more accurately, it marks a turning point in the vast cycle of Earth's slowly changing relationship with our Galaxy. According to Mayan cosmology this cycle lasts 25,626¼ years, and in the next chapter we will explore how this cycle arises. The most important thing is that, from an astronomical perspective, *all that changes is Earth's orientation in Space, in particular its orientation in relation to the Galactic Equator of the Milky Way.*

This changing relationship has many ramifications and possible interpretations of meaning. Simultaneously, many physical changes are occurring on the Earth, some of which are the results of human behaviour affecting global warming; some changes are the result of changing patterns of activity on the Sun, such as fluctuating sunspot and solar flare patterns, and a temporary slowing down of the Sun's 'internal dynamo' currents; some changes may be the result of much larger cycles, as our Solar System moves into a highly charged area of the Galaxy.

In this book, we will explore the significance of these changes to Earth's orientation in Space and the ways in which we as humans are being required to adapt *our* orientation to our inner world, to the world around us, and to our place in the Cosmos and its vast cycles of change. To understand this, we will look at the changes that are being required for Humanity as a whole, as well as for each of us as individuals.

We will explore the major changes, and psychological and spiritual 'shifts' that have occurred over the last 13 years of the Mayan calendar cycle, in ways that will hopefully help to make sense of what has become an increasingly demanding and intensively transformative time. We will also explore what 2012 might require from each of us, according to our astrological Sun Sign.

In particular, we will look at those areas of life where we might need to let go and heal the past, in order to be able to move forward and embrace our true inner purpose. We will explore how to be in 'Right Relationship' with our inner purpose, our relationships, the planet and ourselves.

The most essential change that 2012 brings is a change of inner orientation; we are all being required to turn our focus away from the needs and desires of our personal egos, and to focus attention on understanding and living the inner purpose that arises from within our soul, spirit or essence. At one level, this sounds simple, but it is possibly the most difficult and challenging change that Humanity has undergone in its entire history. The key is that it is an awakening for the *whole of Humanity*, not just a 'chosen few', the 'awakened ones' or the 'ascended ones', but everyone. We are all in this together, and we are getting more and more messages from the Earth, that we can only move through it if we approach it together, as One.

The arrival of 2012 offers everyone on the planet the opportunity for deep and lasting change, by living consciously from the Heart, by moving beyond the fears and delusions of the ego, and by embracing our true potential as co-creators of our destiny. It is up to each of us whether we choose to take up the challenge to awaken to these possibilities. By choosing this path, our way through life will be a whole lot easier.

Chapter 1
EARTH'S PLACE IN THE COSMOS

We live on a planet formed, along with the other planets in our Solar System, over 4.5 billion years ago. After the birth of the Sun, a vast disc of dust and gases, known as the Solar Nebula, remained orbiting the Sun. Over a period of about 20 million years, this Solar Nebula gradually coalesced to form the planets; so, order was formed out of the chaos.

In a very real sense, everything on Earth has a solar origin, from the rocks and minerals to the most complex life forms, including human beings. Everything on Earth was formed from the Solar Nebula, the matter that remained after the birth of our star, the Sun. These discoveries of modern science are now mirroring the ancient wisdom of many indigenous peoples that we all originally come from the stars.

Planet Earth inhabits a vast and varied Solar System, consisting of planets with their moons, asteroids, 'dwarf planets', planetoids and comets. From time immemorial, comets arriving into the inner Solar System have heralded major changes in our consciousness and our world.

Since the deployment of the Hubble Space Telescope in 1990, several new dwarf planets and planetoids have been discovered, orbiting beyond Pluto. The discovery of Sedna in November 2003 increased the distance of known planetary bodies out to 32 times the distance of Neptune from the Sun. Then in January 2005, Eris was discovered, orbiting at nearly twice the distance of Pluto. The discovery of Eris, with a mass 27 per cent larger than Pluto, eventually led to the reclassification by the IAU (International Astronomical Union) of both Pluto and Eris as 'dwarf planets'. However, we should not be fooled by their size; sometimes the smaller a thing is, the more powerful its potential to bring about change – like the mosquito in your sleeping bag!

The planets in the Solar System, from Mercury to Neptune, orbit the Sun in roughly the same orbital plane, (give or take a few degrees to north or south); this is known as the plane of the Ecliptic (see Colour Plate 1). Each planet has its own fixed orbital period around the Sun, ranging from a mere 88 days for Mercury, which is closest to the Sun, to 248 years for Pluto. Now there is Eris, taking 557 years and Sedna a whopping 11,809 years to complete one orbit. It seems that with each new discovery, we are being challenged to extend our perception of the timescales and distances involved in the patterns and behaviour of our neighbours in the Solar System.

It is important to understand that the Solar System behaves as one vast, interconnected organism, with the Sun driving everything from its centre. Each new discovery adds to our understanding of the complex interrelationships of this vast organic whole.

Recent decades have seen a return to the understanding that the Earth is a single organism. This is nothing new; this simple truth has been understood by every ancient culture that the world has ever known. The Earth Mother or Mother Goddess has been depicted in countless ways in various mythologies; she is known in many forms from the Sumerian Ninsun to the

Greeks' Gaia, Cybele and Rhea, to the Celtic Anu, to the Incas' Pachamama, to the Hawaiians' Haumea.

This understanding that the Solar System is also a single organism is only now beginning to emerge. This is changing, with new discoveries about the nature and influence of solar magnetic cycles and the Solar Wind upon *all* the planets in the Solar System. But this, too, was understood in ancient mythologies, where the gods (planets) are usually depicted as parts of one large family, clan or tribe. The mythology, genealogy, dramas and intrigues, which define the relationships between the gods and goddesses and the men, women and children of Earth is more diverse and entertaining than anything that modern TV soap operas have to offer.

Beyond the Earth and the Solar System, we live within the much larger body that is our Galaxy. As we approach the 2012 December Solstice, we are being pushed to remember, understand and appreciate our place within this vast organism.

In the following chapters, we will see how our changing physical relationship with the stars and constellations of our Galaxy, periodically gives rise to changes in our mythology, philosophy, psychology, the evolution of the world's religions and the discoveries of science and technology. Understanding what these changes have meant in the past may enable us to see the present from a different perspective and make sense of the apparent chaos that is occurring in so many different areas of life.

Globally, we are experiencing that chaos at many different levels; from the meltdown of the world's corporate financial systems, climate change and terrorism to the chaos that many are experiencing due to the loss of traditional values of family, community, or systems of religious, spiritual or philosophical belief.

To make sense of all this chaos, let us step back and look at the bigger picture – the *much* bigger picture, of our place within the Galaxy.

Our Place in the Galaxy

Our Solar System lies on the Orion Spur, an outer spiral arm of the Milky Way Galaxy (see Colour Plate 2). The Galaxy is estimated to be between 80,000 and 100,000 light years across; one light year is 670.6 million miles. These vast distances can be hard for us to grasp; to put it more simply, if the Galaxy were 80 miles across, then our Solar System would be just 2 millimetres wide. Our vast and complex Solar System is one tiny cell within the enormous organism of the Galaxy.

The boundaries of the 'cell' of the Solar System are defined by the Heliosphere (see Colour Plate 3). The Heliosphere is like a vast bubble in space formed by the Solar Wind, which streams out plasma and charged particles that are continually being ejected from the surface of the Sun. As the Sun rotates on its axis, the Solar Wind spirals outward in wave-like currents, bathing all the planets of the Solar System with its energy (see Colour Plate 4). The Earth's magnetic field protects the planet and its life forms from the Solar Wind's harmful radiations (see Colour Plate 5).

In December 2010, the Voyager 1 spacecraft, launched by NASA in 1977 to explore the outer Solar System, reached the outer limits of the Heliosphere, at a distance of 10.8 billion miles from the Earth. Voyager's instruments registered that the Solar Wind's velocity had reduced to zero, meaning that Voyager had entered the 'Heliopause', the space between the Heliosphere and interstellar space. Just in time for the transformational date of

2012, a manmade probe, heading in the direction of the Galactic Centre, has reached the outer edge of our Solar System, and preparing to 'boldly go where no one has gone before'.

This important stage in *Voyager's* journey can be seen as a profound symbol of the collective inner journey that Humankind has been on ever since 1977. In November that year the small planetoid Chiron was discovered, orbiting between Saturn and Uranus. Astrologically, Chiron has come to symbolize the quest for personal healing, the return to a wholeness of Spirit and a deep and abiding sense of knowing our place within the whole of Creation. Chiron's 50-year orbit around the Sun shows us at various times how we may heal our sense of separation from the Oneness of Life, the Universe and our spiritual origins.

Whenever a new planet, planetoid or asteroid is discovered, the qualities associated with its mythology begin to emerge from the Unconscious and become more consciously expressed by humanity. This is a mysterious example of what the psychologist C.G. Jung called 'synchronicity'. Richard Tarnas, in *Cosmos and Psyche,* describes it thus: 'Most of us in the course of life have observed coincidences in which two or more independent events having no apparent causal connection, nevertheless seem to form a meaningful pattern. On occasion, this patterning can strike one as so extraordinary that it is difficult to believe the coincidence has been produced by chance alone. The events give the distinct impression of having been precisely arranged, invisibly orchestrated.'[1]

The discovery of Uranus in 1781 (with a telescope) coincided with an upsurge in the development and use of science and technology. It came toward the culmination of the Age of Enlightenment, which had swept away many old power structures, traditional beliefs and ways of thinking about the world. Uranus' astrological meaning is concerned with going beyond the boundaries of the known world, enabling us to think in ways that break new ground, discover new ways of doing things and new ways of perceiving the Universe. Uranus' discovery also coincided with the closing stages of the American War of Independence, heralding the birth of a powerful, technologically advanced culture that was to dominate the world stage for the next 200 or more years.

The discovery of Neptune in 1846 coincided with an upsurge of interest in alternatives to traditional religions. One of the most notable was Spiritualism, which led to the establishment of the Theosophical Movement in 1875 and brought the spiritual teachings of the East to the attention of the West. Fifty years after Neptune's discovery came the development of psychoanalysis by Freud, Jung and others. Neptune is concerned with what is nebulous and indefinable, with matters of the Unconscious and the Spirit. It is similar to Uranus in that it takes us beyond the realms of the known. Whereas Uranus does this through the mind, Neptune does it through the feelings. Neptune enables us to 'feel into' the truth of any situation and to merge our awareness with something greater than ourselves. The tricky part is being able to distinguish between truth and illusion, which is the challenge when we begin to dissolve our ego's boundaries and experience the reality of something greater than ourselves. Neptune can inspire us and reveal to us the mysteries of the Universe, or it can lead us into realms of fantasy, wishful thinking or delusion.

Chiron's discovery in 1977 coincided with the exponential growth of the spiritual awareness movement in the West, with the emergence into the mainstream of systems of traditional and alternative medicine, Yoga, T'ai Ch'i, etc. In the late 1970's, the environmental movement also went global with the establishment of Greenpeace International, which was largely responsible for kick-starting global concern about many of the most pressing environmental issues, which are now considered mainstream.

We will see how Chiron has played a crucial role in the process of individual and global healing, preparing us all for the changes that are occurring.

A Change of Perspective

Colour Plate 6 shows our perspective on the Galaxy, looking in toward the central hub of stars at the Galactic Centre. The central line of the Milky Way is known as the 'Galactic Equator', and is indicated by the white line. The Ecliptic plane of the Solar System is inclined at an angle of about 60° in relation to the Galactic Plane (indicated by the red line). This means that when we look at the night sky, we see the Milky Way apparently inclined at an angle of 60° in relation to us (see Colour Plate 8).

Lying along the centre of the Galactic Equator, very close to the Galactic Centre is an area known as the Dark Rift. The Maya of Central America knew this as the *Xibalba-be,* which translates as 'road to the underworld'; it is perceived as the birth canal of the Cosmic Mother, leading right into the heart of the Galactic Centre.

Just as everything in our Solar System is fuelled by the energy of the Sun, so does the central hub of the Galaxy drive the movement of the Galaxy. This is the area of the Galaxy where hundreds of new stars are born, roughly every 500 million years; it is quite literally the heart of creation. At the centre of the hub, there is thought to be a supermassive black hole, formed by the intense gravitational forces of the Galactic Centre (GC), pulling into itself all of the material from the old, dying stars of that region. The gravity of a black hole is so dense that not even light can escape.

Precessional Change

From the perspective of the Earth, the Sun appears to gradually change its position in relation to the background of the stars over a period of time. This gradual shifting is particularly noticeable, and relevant, at the crucial turning points of the year – the Equinoxes and Solstices – and is known as the Precession of the Equinoxes. Precession will be explained more fully in the next chapter.

As a result of Precession, the December Solstice Sun has appeared to be traversing the Dark Rift on the Galactic Equator since 1986. Thirteen years later, on 22 December 1999, it had reached the deepest part of the Dark Rift. Thirteen years after that, on 21 December 2012, the Solstice Sun will begin to emerge from the centre of the Dark Rift, symbolically reborn out of the galactic Womb of Creation.

Every year, the Winter Solstice is a time of descent into darkness and stillness, in preparation for a spiritual rebirth. In the yearly cycle of the Earth around the Sun, 21–22 December is the time when the Earth's Northern Hemisphere reaches its maximum tilt away from the Sun. The Sun reaches its lowest point in the sky and the days are shortest. At the same time, it is the Southern Hemisphere's Summer Solstice. In the north, it appears that the Sun descends into the Earth, before being 'reborn' after the Winter Solstice, bringing the promise, potential and hope that accompanies every new birth.

The significance of the Midwinter Sun emerging from the centre of the Dark Rift of the Galactic Equator is profound. This

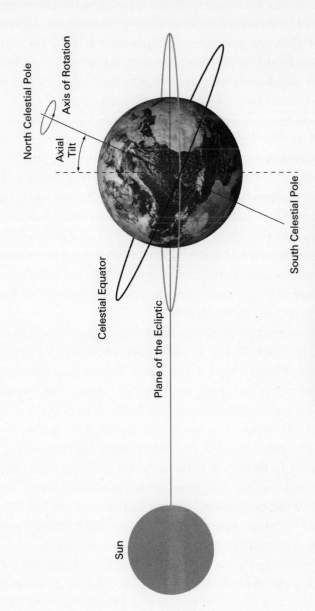

North Celestial Pole

Axis of Rotation

Axial
Tilt

Celestial Equator

Plane of the Ecliptic

South Celestial Pole

Sun

Earth's Tilt at Northern Winter/Southern Summer Solstice
Adapted from a picture by Dennis Nilsson; Earth image from istockphoto.com

alignment only occurs every 25,626 years. It is the emergence of a huge new creative impulse, flowing from the very centre of the Galaxy. As this energy of Galactic rebirth aligns with the yearly rebirth of the Winter Solstice, it creates a direct link between our Earthly (physical) origins, our Solar (spiritual) origins and our Galactic (cosmic or divine) origins.

Light from the Galactic Centre takes roughly 26,000 years to reach us. This means that the New Light that is emerging into our consciousness in 2012 began its journey toward us at the beginning of the last Midwinter Sun alignment with the Galactic Equator 25,626 years ago. For the last half of this 26,000-year cycle (13,000 years), the Midwinter Sun has been traversing the southern hemisphere of the Galaxy. This has taken our consciousness into ever deepening levels of duality and materialism. This polarization of opposites reached its most extreme during the last 2,000 years of the Age of Pisces, which is the zodiac constellation that lies closest to the Galactic South Pole.

To appreciate the significance of this, it helps to understand something about Chakras or energy centres. According to the traditions of Indian Yoga, Chinese and Tibetan mysticism and many other spiritual traditions, there are seven main energy centres, or vortices, in the human body. These lie in the central line, from the crown of the head to the base of the body; they are commonly referred to by their Sanskrit name *Chakra,* meaning 'wheel'. The further down in the body, the more polarized their energy becomes; so, the Crown Chakra connects us with the oneness of the spirit, while the Root Chakra connects us to the polarized world of opposites – female and male, physical and spiritual, light and dark, conscious and unconscious, etc.

If we approach the Galaxy as a single organism, then it seems that this too has energy centres or Chakras. At its heart lies the vast hub of stars at the Galactic Centre. The North Pole

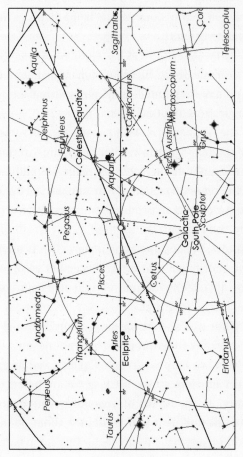

The Galactic South Pole

Image Produced by Chris Marriott's SkyMap Pro

of the Galaxy is like the Galactic Crown Centre, and the South Pole of the Galaxy is the Galactic Root Centre. In the human body, it is the Root Centre that connects us most strongly with the physical and material aspects of our being. So, while we have been traversing the Age of Pisces, this has taken us into the most polarized expressions of our being, with extremes of physicality and spirituality.

This is why the Age of Pisces has required so many spiritual teachers, for example Jesus, Buddha, Mohammed, who each, in their own way, have reminded us of our spiritual origins and that we originate from the One Light.

During the final years leading up to 2012, we have witnessed the gradual breakdown and dissolution of much that we have been taught to perceive as reality. Simultaneously, everyone on the planet, consciously or unconsciously, is being led through a process of remembering our spiritual origins. In order for us to fully reawaken, we need to release all old fears, opinions, attitudes, beliefs, and attachments. This is an ongoing process; it does not mean that on 22 December 2012 everyone on the planet will suddenly become enlightened, although some seem genuinely to believe that.

It is only our ego and its physical, emotional and mental attachments that make this process challenging. This is about letting go so that we may wake up as gently and as easily as possible. This is no simple task because we are being required to let go of literally thousands of years of negative emotional attachments, confusion, fear and ignorance about our spiritual origins. We don't really have a choice, however; the bottom line is that we are all being swept along by these irresistible energies of change.

Whether we believe in reincarnation or not makes no difference. If we take the view that we evolve over many lifetimes in order to bring all aspects of our consciousness into an inner alignment and harmony, then we will have experienced every aspect of human experience and the whole gamut of emotional and physical attachments. If, on the other hand, we believe that we are just here for the one time, that this life is all that there is, then we are still subject to the inherited patterns of our DNA, and to our collective ancestral and cultural memory. At an unconscious level, we are still dealing with the spiritual, mythological and psychological heritage that has evolved over hundreds of thousands of years.

Waking up from this dream (or illusion) must be a gradual, step-by-step process if we are to negotiate it in a way that allows for the integration of our spiritual, mental, emotional and physical self. Anything else will create imbalance, confusion and delusion, and perpetuate the split between physical and spiritual consciousness, which is precisely what is trying to heal.

We can see this process at work in the world at this very moment. It is clear that there are unprecedented changes taking place at every level. The old structures and institutions – governments, religions, banks, etc – and the belief systems and thought patterns that underpin them are clearly breaking down. Efforts to support these crumbling structures are either becoming more frantic and extreme, or moving into denial.

All of this is to be expected as we approach the change of an age. Every time Earth has moved from one Great Age to another, there has been disruption, confusion and fear of the unknown. We know what happened at the end of the Taurean Age and the beginning of the Arien Age, as Moses led the Israelites out of Egypt. This heralded the end of the power of the Egyptian dynasties, and the development of a monotheistic religion in Judaism. Moses became the strong, powerful leader and instigator of the Age of Aries, bringing its new rules for living in the form of the Ten Commandments, which he used to destroy the Golden Calf, the symbol of the dying Age of Taurus the Bull.

Two thousand years later, at the end of the Age of Aries, Jesus was born in Bethlehem. Three Zoroastrian priest-king-astrologers from Persia came to pay him homage, and to pass the baton from the previous age. Within days, Herod ordered the murder of all the first-born in Bethlehem, in an attempt to destroy the bringer of this New Age of Pisces, right at its outset. This was a time of turbulence, oppression and chaos. The Romans were occupying the land of Israel, and there was dissatisfaction, anger and acts of terrorism. It all sounds rather familiar, doesn't it?

All of this is a consequence of the new energies, archetypes and ideals as they emerge to take root at the beginning of a New Age. This process was summed up by Jesus in his simple, poetic approach when he said that 'you cannot put the new wine into old wineskins'[2], as this contaminates the new wine. The 'new wine' refers to the new teachings and frequencies of a New Age. This saying is as relevant now, as we enter the Age of Aquarius, as it was then at the beginning of the Age of Pisces.

Even when we begin to release ourselves from our old patterns and beliefs, we are still trying to grasp the new Aquarian teachings, ideals, mythology and spirituality from the perspective of our old, Age of Pisces psychology and mentality; this causes much confusion, and ungrounded thinking. It is little wonder that many people are suspicious or dismissive of the 'New Age', when many of its ideas appear to be often quite literally off the planet. Vagueness and ungroundedness result from only a partial grasping of true Aquarian ideals, which are still being interpreted and expressed in very Piscean Age ways.

Examples range from the prophets of doom approach, such as the illusory millennium bug (which meant that everything would stop working at midnight on 1 January 2000), to those who have reassured us that we are all about to be miraculously saved from our human follies by extraterrestrials from Sirius, the Pleiades, or elsewhere.

Until we are completely free from the Piscean Age psychological archetypes and move more fully into the Aquarian Age, there are few who will be able to fully grasp its true meaning with any degree of clarity. There are various levels of understanding and sensing that Aquarius is concerned with brotherhood, sisterhood and collective responsibility, while respecting the needs of the individual. There is also an awareness that it is about reawakening to our full spiritual potential and to express this in the physical world in harmonious and mutually supportive and nurturing ways. We are already seeing the perceptions and language of mysticism and quantum physics becoming almost indistinguishable but there is a long way to go before these ideas filter down into day-to-day awareness.

If we can be inspired by the true impulse of the Age of Aquarius, while remaining grounded, we will be able to vision and create a better future, without getting lost in fantasy. After December 2012, the consciousness shift will increase at an exponential rate. It is beyond belief, however, that we will all wake up on 22 December 2012 to find that we have all ascended, or that the world's drug barons and mafia suddenly see the error of their ways, the world's politicians see the light, oil companies decide to give away their profits, and investment bankers decide that they will all donate their bonuses to the poor.

Nor is it likely that the consciousness of the planet will be split in some way, so that the more advanced souls will go on to live a life of spiritual bliss and happiness, untroubled by all of the negativity and chaos. Meanwhile other lesser mortals will be left to wallow in a world of struggle and pain. That sounds like the old dualistic belief in Heaven and Hell, wrapped up in New Age jargon. That belief stems from a Piscean Age perpetuation of duality and the split between physical and spiritual consciousness. It is not Aquarian in any sense of the word.

The astrological glyph for Aquarius is ≈≈ and it holds the key to understanding this, as it shows the energetic relationship of 'As Above, So Below'. Long before this saying was inscribed above the temples of ancient Greece, this universal symbol for energy was carved into several of the world's ancient megalithic structures, particularly in the passage tombs of Ireland and Carnac in Brittany. The symbol was used to show where Earth energy is particularly strong.

The Aquarian symbol represents congruity and harmony between the spiritual and physical worlds; a developing understanding of their true relationship, based on clarity of thinking and feeling, and freed from any divisive dogma, which has distorted the world's major spiritual teachings for so long.

One of the great dilemmas facing us is how to keep an open heart, while maintaining discernment. In order to truly perceive spiritual truth or reality, our heart has to be open; we cannot grasp such realities with our minds alone. Spiritual teachers throughout the ages have known and taught this. It is the discerning faculty of the mind, however, that enables us to sort and separate what is true and has meaning, from all the many illusions, half-truths or distortions that can abound. When we are open-hearted we are more likely to accept things without judgment; but open-heartedness without discernment can make us more gullible and open to deception.

So, it is important to maintain a constant dialogue between our open hearts and our discerning minds. No matter how much our heart may want to believe that something is true, or that we are perceiving a spiritual reality, a physical manifestation of a spiritual being, or any number of wonderful things, it is *always* important to do a reality check on such experiences, so that we do not allow our open-heartedness to make us gullible.

Similarly, it is important not to allow our discerning or critical minds to negate the reality of our spiritual experiences, insights and the inner 'knowing' of our hearts. This is a constant balancing act at which we all need to become more proficient. At times we may fall off balance, but each time we do, we can learn to hone this crucial relationship between heart and mind, so that we may reach a truer perception of what we see around us and within us.

So, you are urged to read on with an open heart, but not to simply accept what is written here as 'the truth'. It should be tested against your own inner knowing and spiritual discernment, and sometimes it will be necessary to check the 'facts' or insights, as they are written, to see if they can be corroborated.

Everything written here has been researched and tested in this way, and sources are quoted in the Chapter Notes. This book, however is an attempt to weave together many strands from different disciplines, such as astrology, astronomy, ancient wisdom teachings, quantum physics, Earth mysteries as well as personal inner experience and inner 'knowing'. Sometimes the connections that are made may seem obvious, at others they may not immediately make sense, but may gradually begin to do so. At other times, you may feel that they are just too far-fetched to be true. If that is the case, then it is important not to simply accept it anyway, but to test it, check it and maybe reject it.

The real truth is that no one on this planet truly knows what will happen in December 2012. Even the present day Mayan elders do not claim to know; many discarnate or 'Ascended Masters' of spiritual wisdom say that they do not know. What will manifest after 21 December 2012 is dependent upon the choices that we make and the actions that we take, individually and collectively. What follows is a best shot at making sense of it all, offered with the spirit of love and the hope that it may help to make your journey more enjoyable, understandable, inspiring and uplifting.

CHAPTER 2

PRECESSION AND THE MAYAN LONG COUNT CALENDAR

The Mayan Long Count Calendar was probably formulated between 354 BCE and CE 41 in the region of Izapa, Mexico[1]. Although its calculations extend back much further in time, this is the first era with monuments that actually depict this calendar.

The Long Count divides the precessional cycle of 25,626¼ years into five Suns, each lasting 5,125¼ years. The current Sun began on 13 August 3114 BCE and will end on 21 December 2012 (some say 23 December). Each Sun consists of 13 Baktuns, each lasting 144,000 days (394¼ years).

Each 5,125¼-year Sun carries a different polarity, the first four cycles alternating between feminine and masculine. The cycle due to end on 21 December 2012 was a masculine, patriarchal cycle; the new Fifth Sun cycle will create a balance between the feminine and the masculine. In order for this to occur, we each need to focus on creating a balance between the male and female within us, in all of our dealings with each other and with the Earth herself. This is the true meaning of moving into Right Relationship.

The Sun shifts its precessional position by only 1° every 72 years, and the Maya developed sophisticated ways to observe the subtle changes in the positions of the stars over very long periods, to arrive at such an accurate precessional calendar.

Precession

In the West, the discovery of Precession is attributed to Aristarchus of Samos (280 BCE), or Hipparchus of Rhodes (147 BCE). As the Earth rotates on its axis, it wobbles slowly, like a gyroscope or spinning top; this gradually changes the alignment of the North and South Poles in relation to the stars. According to the latest Solar System research, the complete precessional cycle takes about 25,700 years[2] – just 74 years' difference (just over 1°) to the Mayan Long Count calculation.

Polar Precession Relative to the Stars

Colour Plate 9 shows the present position of the rotational North Pole, aligned with Polaris, the Pole Star; Colour Plate 10 shows how, by CE 14,000 the rotational North Pole will have moved to align near Vega, in the constellation Lyra.

As we stand on the Earth looking upward (as shown in Colour Plate 9), the axis appears to move counter-clockwise across the sky. So, the precessional movement seems to go against the Earth's direction of rotation. The wobble is due to the gravitational pulls of the Sun and Moon creating a 'torque effect' on the Earth.

Looked at from energetic, symbolic and mythological levels, this means that a tension is constantly played out between the physical (Earth) plane, the emotional (Lunar) plane, the mental (Solar) plane and the spiritual or celestial Galactic plane. This 'torque tension' and the gradual changes that it brings in the relationship between the Earth, Moon, Sun and stars result in the slowly changing cycles of the Great Ages. In some mysterious way, these physical and energetic changes influence us at the psychological and spiritual levels.

It appears that our changing orientation to the stars, or starlight, influences how we experience the spiritual and psychological 'archetypes of the Unconscious'[3]. Even a very basic exploration of the history of mythology reveals that these changes have influenced the mythological archetypes of the past, and their accompanying spiritual and religious beliefs. These changing patterns are explored in great depth in the scholarly book *Hamlet's Mill*[4]; for now, we will just consider the basics of this relationship between the stars and the human unconscious.

The Changing Equinoxes

As well as shifting Earth's orientation at the Poles, precession causes the Equinoxes and Solstices to move backward in relation to the zodiac constellations. So, the zodiac constellations that lie beyond the Spring and Autumn Equinox points change approximately every 2,135 years – hence 'Precession of the Equinoxes'. This will be easier to understand from the diagrams on pages 23 and 24.

Earth's rotational axis is tilted about 23½° in relation to its path around the Sun (the Ecliptic); this tilt gives rise to the changing seasons. Earth's equator extended out into space is called the 'Celestial Equator'. The Equinoxes occur when the Sun reaches the point where the Celestial Equator intersects with the plane of the Ecliptic (see Colour Plate 11).

While the basic patterns of the seasons, defined by the Equinoxes and Solstices, are largely unchanging, their physical and mythological characteristics gradually change over millennia, due to Precessional shift. We can see this quite clearly if we look at the position of the Northern Hemisphere Spring Equinox Sun at the beginning of the Age of Pisces, around CE 6 (see page 23).

Then if we look at the Sun's position at Spring Equinox in 2012 (see page 24), we see that it has almost completely traversed the constellation of Pisces, and is moving toward the stars of Aquarius – hence the approaching 'Age of Aquarius'.

The Two Zodiacs – Tropical and Sidereal

To fully appreciate what occurs at the December Solstice in 2012, it is essential to understand the relationship between the Tropical Zodiac and the Sidereal Zodiac. It is worthwhile spending some time getting to grips with this, so please do not be tempted to skip over this part.

In traditional astrology, the point of intersection between the Celestial Equator and the Ecliptic marks the Spring Equinox in the Northern Hemisphere, and defines the beginning of the Tropical Zodiac at 0° Aries (see Colour Plate 11). This remains so, even though due to Precession, the Sidereal Zodiac stars of the constellation of Pisces are actually in the background, behind the Spring Equinox point (see Colour Plate 12).

It is like a wheel within a wheel. The relationship between the Celestial Equator and the Ecliptic defines where the Equinoxes and

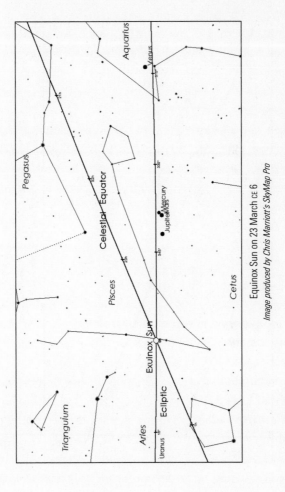

Equinox Sun on 23 March CE 6

Image produced by Chris Marriott's SkyMap Pro

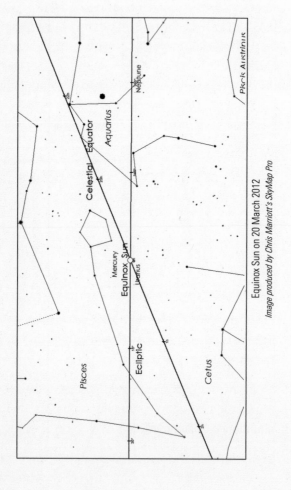

Equinox Sun on 20 March 2012

Image produced by Chris Marriott's SkyMap Pro

Solstices occur: the 360° Tropical Zodiac has 12 equal divisions, so that each Tropical Zodiac sign is 30°. Summer Solstice occurs when the Sun is at 0° Cancer, the Autumn Equinox at 0° Libra, and the Winter Solstice at 0° Capricorn. The 12 equal Tropical Zodiac divisions are used to define the changing processes and seasonal cycles of growth during the year; they do not accurately reflect the actual sizes or positions of the constellations of stars, known as the Sidereal Zodiac.

The Tropical Zodiac is a mental construct that is the basis of Western astrology. The meanings of the 12 seasonal Tropical Zodiac divisions have remained unchanged, despite the gradual precessional shift of the constellations in the background. These meanings are derived from the regular yearly cycle of Earth's movement around the Sun:

- Tropical Aries (beginning at Spring Equinox) is the time of new beginnings;

- Tropical Taurus is the time for consolidation, stability and growth that follows;

- Tropical Gemini is the time to draw in new information, energy and substance, enabling growth to continue;

- Tropical Cancer (beginning at Summer Solstice) brings the rich fullness of the growth cycle and the abundance of summer;

- Tropical Leo is the time of allowing the ripening of all our creative efforts and relaxing into the enjoyment of the summer warmth;

- Tropical Virgo is the beginning of the harvest, when we begin to see the fruits of our efforts in all areas of life;

- Tropical Libra (beginning at Autumn Equinox) is a time of balance and stillness, before the gradual withdrawal of energy in the autumn;

- Tropical Scorpio is when everything begins to decay and withdraws back into the depths of the Earth, putting back the nutrients, which will further the growth of the next cycle;

- Tropical Sagittarius is the time for appraising what has passed, and formulating the vision for what will come in the next cycle;

- Tropical Capricorn (beginning at Winter Solstice) is when everything has withdrawn into the Earth, gathering energy, substance and resources in anticipation of the next cycle;

- Tropical Aquarius is the time when we can make concrete plans how to apply our vision and best use our resources, as we approach the new spring;

- Tropical Pisces is the time for releasing our attachments, or any unresolved feelings about the previous cycle, so that we can emerge renewed and cleansed at the beginning of the new cycle at Spring Equinox.

The psychological and spiritual meanings that have become attributed to the Tropical Zodiac have their roots in our ancestors' dependence for all their needs on the repeating yearly cycle of Nature.

Around 4,000 years ago, when the roots of Western astrology were developing in Sumeria, the stars that lay behind the Spring Equinox (Tropical Zodiac) point were in the constellation (Sidereal Zodiac) of Aries. So, at that time, the Tropical and Sidereal zodiacs were congruent. As we have seen, precessional shift has caused the two zodiacs to move out of synch with each other. From the perspective of our normal awareness and our relationship with the natural cycles of the year, the meanings of the Tropical Zodiac signs remain valid. When we start to consider deeper spiritual and archetypal patterns, however, then we need to look more closely at the Sidereal Zodiac constellations.

There are many levels of influence. It is obvious that our immediate environment has an influence upon us and upon our behaviour, even though not everyone born into the same family, neighbourhood, town or country will behave and react to that environment in the same way. Some may become victims of circumstance whereas others may develop great strength of character and achieve great things.

Factors such as DNA, upbringing and education all play their parts. Beyond that, there are personal and collective beliefs and attitudes, social conscience and our internal reactions toward the world in general. In addition, there are our unconscious patterns, some inherited from parents and family, and some just inherent in our nature. Then, we can choose to extend our frame of reference to include conscious or unconscious past life memories. Finally, there are the effects of the larger environment – our place on Earth, and Earth's place in relation to the Universe.

Some argue that the influences coming from beyond the Earth are too subtle to be discernible, compared to the influence of environment, DNA and upbringing. The more we learn about the powerful energetic connections between Sun and Earth, however, the weaker this argument becomes. If we observe the effects that increased sunspot activity and solar magnetic storms can have upon human emotions and behaviour, and even stock markets, it is clear that what happens in space has a profound influence.

When we take into account the subtle energetic qualities and relationships between all the planets and the Sun, then a whole different picture emerges. This phenomena has been graphically and beautifully described in *The Disappearance of the Universe* by Gary Renard (p183)[5]:

> 'Let's say you could look at (the) planet from outer space, from half the distance to the Moon, and that you could see chi (energy). You'd then be able to see that the Earth is completely encased by electromagnetic chi that's carried to it, and past it, in the form of a huge flow of radiation from the Sun. This flow of chi is constantly changing, with yin and yang going in and out of balance and everywhere in between balanced. The changes in the chi are caused, in turn, by the constantly changing radiation of the sun.
>
> Now, if you could look at the Sun close up from space, you'd see what could be described as enormous swirling oceans of gas. What few realize is that these oceans of gas behave in a similar fashion to the oceans of the Earth. Just as the tides of the Earth's oceans are subject to the movements of (the) Moon, the tides of those Solar Oceans of gas are subject to the pulling and pushing of the total interaction of all of the planets in (the) Solar System, and even the Universe beyond it – which of course is all connected. This causes different gaseous tides, sunspots and other solar events – which in turn regulate the changes in the flow of the radiation while it's carried to the Earth as particles via the Solar Wind, or directly by sunlight.

This changing radiational flow, regulated by the movement within the entire Solar System, including the Earth and its Moon, causes corresponding changes in the chi surrounding the planet and sends electromagnetic fields into every inch of it. You can't see these chi electromagnetic fields with the body's eyes, but they're everywhere – and you've been walking right through them every day of your life. They regulate everything about you, including your decisions and resulting movements. They are actually thought from a completely different level, transmuted into the form of chi, telling you what to think on this level. Everything you do follows from what you think, and sometimes it follows instantly, like a reflex.'

The Constellations and Changing Ages

Aries is a relatively small constellation; the Age of Aries, during which time the Spring Equinox point passed in front of its stars, began around 1700 BCE and lasted until the birth of Jesus (CE 6/7). Jesus was one of the world teachers who inaugurated the change from the Age of Aries to the Age of Pisces; the development of early Christianity was rich with fish symbolism. Many of the disciples were fishermen, and Jesus said he would make them 'fishers of men' (Mark 1:16–20); there are the miracles of the draught of fishes, and of the loaves and the fishes. The latter refers to the relationship between the opposite signs of Virgo (the corn mother) and Pisces (the fishes). The early Christians in Rome used the fish symbol as a means of identification. This symbol has enjoyed a revival in recent years, although many who use it might not appreciate that its origins lie in astrology.

Pisces is often depicted as two fishes swimming in opposite directions, symbolizing the polarization of matter and spirit that has dominated the last 2,000 years. At its best, Pisces is capable of spiritual devotion and transcendence, but it can also lead into a world of illusion, delusion and wishful thinking. The Age of Pisces enabled us to experience the extreme polarities within our nature, from the most sublime spiritual experiences to the deepest immersion in the desires of the material world. As we approach the end of this Age, it sometimes appears that there is an ever-increasing divide between the spiritual and the material.

For many, disillusionment with traditional religions has led to a complete rejection of the spiritual and an immersion in material values, or brought about a search for deeper meaning and a hunger for direct spiritual experience. For some, the uncertainties and changing energies of the times have resulted in ever more entrenched, dogmatic or fundamentalist viewpoints, in a desperate attempt to cling to something definite and certain. These perspectives are all products of the changing and chaotic energies of the time, as we try to negotiate the changeover from the Age of Pisces to Aquarius.

At this time of upheaval, change and chaos, it is essential to address our inner emotional and mental chaos and fears; only when we acknowledge these can we develop mental discernment and spiritual compassion. We can then respond positively to the various dramas that unfold daily around us, moving away from feelings of powerlessness into taking our place as co-creators of the future.

We have seen how the Tropical Zodiac is based on the energetic cycles arising from the Equinoxes and the Solstices; it is like a girdle of energies around and within the Earth's magnetic field. The Tropical Zodiac begins at the equinoctial point (0° Aries), where the Ecliptic and Celestial Equator intersect, while the background of the stars (Sidereal Zodiac) slowly changes in relation to this.

With the Sidereal Zodiac constellations, we are looking at star patterns and energies many light years away from our Solar System; their light and energy takes thousands of years to reach us. We know from modern technologies that light carries information – this is how fibre optics work, how the Internet works, and so on. We know from astronomy that the light spectrum emanating from a star or a planet can tell us about the chemical composition of that body.

It seems that the light frequencies and information carried by the light of different stars, forming the constellations familiar to us, somehow act upon the deeper levels of our unconscious mind. We then project images, thoughts and feelings onto those star patterns, creating our own stories, which influence the unfolding of human history, philosophy, religion, knowledge and technology. There is a profound mystery at work here: why is it that the light and frequencies from stars, often thousands of light years away from each other, should have such a profound influence on our human mythology, psychology and spirituality?

When we look at the mythologies from each Great Age we begin to get an inkling of the mysterious and powerful forces at work. There are many examples of cultures on opposite sides of the world having remarkably similar myths, associated with particular star patterns. To the objective, rational mind this makes no sense and it is easy to dismiss these myths as imagination, wishful thinking, projection or the attempts of so-called 'primitive' minds to make sense of the Universe. But even cursory examination of the world's great creation myths reveals too many uncanny similarities in world myths, their relationships with the stars, and their influence on individual and collective archetypes within the human unconscious.

Spring Equinox 1700 BCE – Age of Aries

The diagram on page 33 shows the Sun at the intersection of the Ecliptic and the Celestial Equator, with the first stars of Aries in the background, at the beginning of the Age of Aries around 1700 BCE.

Notice how the stars of Aries and Taurus overlap, causing confusion between the ages. This time period was described in the story of Moses, an initiator of the Age of Aries, who led a nation out of captivity in Egypt, on a long journey through the desert to the Promised Land. Moses went up Mount Sinai to receive the new Laws for the Age of Aries, which we know as the Ten Commandments. When he came down from the mountain he found that many of the Israelites had reverted to the worship of the Golden Calf, a symbol of the religion of the dying Age of Taurus.

Ancient Greek mythology also refers to this time in the story of Theseus and the Minotaur. Theseus slew the Minotaur, a beast that was half man/half bull, illustrating his role as an initiator of the change from Taurus to Aries. There are several other myths in Middle Eastern cultures about bull-slayers, among them Gilgamesh, Gayomart and the Persian Mithra, later adopted by the Romans as Mithras.

The mythology of the Age of Aries (c.1700 BCE to CE 6/7) was dominated by the symbolism of the Ram, or Lamb. In Greek mythology we find reference back to this age in the heroic quest of Jason and the Argonauts to recover the Golden Fleece, which represents the redemptive and healing qualities of Aries.

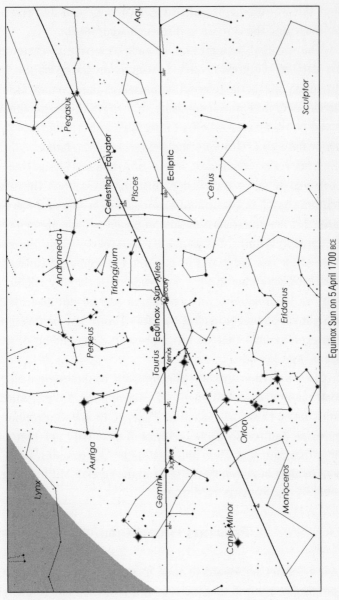

Equinox Sun on 5 April 1700 BCE
Image Produced by Chris Marriott's SkyMap Pro

From the Age of Aries we also find the origins of the stories about the warrior heroes of Ancient Greece, such as Perseus, who overcame the Gorgon and rescued Andromeda.

The spiritual inaugurators of each New Age consistently refer back to the previous age as well as preparing us for the subsequent age. Jesus referred to himself as the 'Lamb of God'; whereas everyone was expecting an Aries-like warrior-king, instead he was a man who had integrated and transformed the warrior nature of Aries into the gentleness of the lamb.

After Jesus' crucifixion, Joseph of Arimathea (Jesus' uncle) is believed to have travelled to Britain to establish the first Christian church in Glastonbury, now said to be one of the main centres for the Aquarian Age. Joseph is said to have planted the original Holy Thorn of Glastonbury on Wearyall Hill, the site of one of the two fishes of Pisces in the Glastonbury Landscape Zodiac[6]. In December 2010, a 'descendant' of the original Holy Thorn on Wearyall Hill was vandalized and all but destroyed. The removal of the 'crown' of the Holy Thorn may be taken as a powerful symbol that we are approaching the ending of the Piscean Age.

However, there are other descendants of the original Holy Thorn planted in the Gardens of Glastonbury Abbey, which nestles just below the Aquarian Phoenix in the Glastonbury Landscape Zodiac. So while the symbol of the old age may be dying, that thread is alive and well under the watchful eye of the Glastonbury Zodiac Phoenix of Aquarius.

Previous Great Ages

Moving further backward in time to explore the mythologies of prehistory, we find that the symbolism of each age is always consistent with the qualities of the predominant Sidereal Zodiac constellation. In the Age of Taurus (approximately 4542–1700 BCE), almost everywhere we look there are Bull-cults.

It is important to remember that the dates of the Great Ages depend on the actual position of the Equinoctial points in relation to the background of the stars. This is a natural, organic and real process; it is not a mental construct, dividing the Great Ages into twelve equal divisions of the total 25,626 years. Some zodiac constellations, like Taurus, are much longer than others, such as Cancer; hence their ages last for corresponding periods of time.

Barring any radical shift in the Earth's rotational tilt in the next several years, the Spring Equinox point will not actually completely clear the stars of Pisces until around CE 2600. So, we still have quite a while to go before we can say that we have arrived in the Age of Aquarius, uncontaminated by the old paradigms and archetypes of the Piscean Age. It is an ongoing and drawn-out process of birth occurring in several stages. December 2012 is just one, albeit very important, stage in this vast unfolding cycle of change.

The Iron and Bronze Ages

During the recent astrological ages, developments in human civilization and technology correspond with the qualities of each age. The Iron Age proper began around 1300 BCE, about 700 years into the Age of Aries. Aries is ruled by the planet Mars, which is traditionally associated with iron, and it is believed that Mars has an iron core, like the Earth. There is evidence of the use of iron implements before that, as far back as 4000 BCE. However, at that time only small objects like spear tips and ornaments were made from iron that was recovered from meteorites – iron from space.

If we go back further to the Bronze Age, we find that although it developed at different times in different continents, it was first used in the Middle East, then Central and Western Asia and south-east Europe around 4000 BCE, at the beginning of the Age of Taurus.

The ruling planet of Taurus is Venus, and her traditional metal is copper. In central Europe, the use of copper by the Beaker people had become common by about 3300 BCE – about 700 years into the Taurean Age. As this Age developed, the use of copper was very quickly combined with tin, to create the alloy Bronze, which is of course much more enduring than copper.

The Bronze Age continued well into the Age of Aries, overlapping the Iron Age. In Britain the Bronze Age is considered to run from about 2100–700 BCE, thus spanning both of these two Great Ages.

Age of Taurus

The Spring Equinox of 4490 BCE was highly significant; there was an exact conjunction of the Sun and Venus, the ruling planet of Taurus and, due to the precessional shift, the Spring Equinox point was also exactly aligned with the Galactic Equator (see page 37). This marked the beginning of the Age of Taurus.

It heralded a time of physical and spiritual harmony, new beginnings at a cosmic galactic level, at a spiritual solar level, and at the human emotional level. In the human body, Venus resonates most strongly with the solar plexus, the energy centre

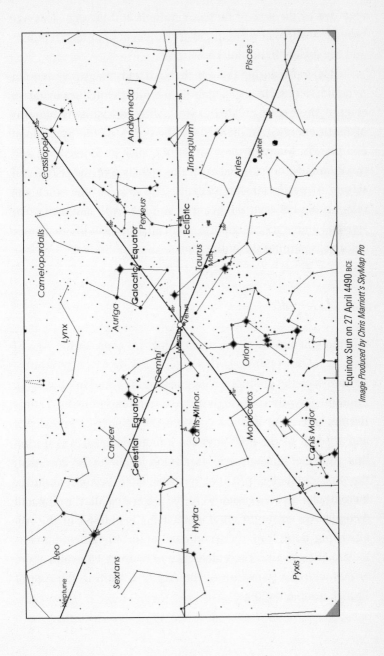

Equinox Sun on 27 April 4490 BCE

Image Produced by Chris Marriott's SkyMap Pro

regarded as the seat of human emotions and the ego. This age brought a whole new era in the development of human relations and the dissemination of knowledge.

It was also during this age that vast and complex systems of pyramids, stone circles, megaliths and other structures began to emerge; these were created to work with the changing patterns of Earth energies, influenced by the cycles of the Sun, Moon and planets. Many of these structures, such as Stonehenge and the Pyramids, are aligned with the planets and the rising and setting of particular star systems. This was an age when the relationship between the heavens and the Earth assumed great spiritual and practical importance in all aspects of life in diverse cultures, spanning the entire globe.

Age of Gemini

Moving still further backward in time, we come to the Age of Gemini (6500–4490 BCE). This Age, ruled by Mercury (Thoth-Hermes) saw the gradual development and evolution of writing. From the Egyptians through to the Greeks and Romans, Thoth-Hermes (Mercury) has always been the bringer of knowledge and wisdom of the gods into the human realm. It was during this Age that ancient oral traditions began to be recorded; the first symbolic, pictorial systems later become complex hieroglyphs and eventually forms of script that we would recognize as writing. *Cuneiform* script, the oldest known form of writing, dates from the second half of the 4th millennium BCE, in Sumeria; so the true emergence of writing coincides more or less with the transition of the Age of Gemini to the Age of Taurus, around 4490 BCE.

Age of Cancer – Dawn of 'Western Civilization'

Going still further back, we arrive at the so-called beginning of western civilization, which emerged in Asia Minor during the Age of Cancer (7900–6500 BCE). This age saw the movement from nomadic hunter-gathering to established agriculture, the ascendancy of ancient Goddess religions, and the eventual establishment of the first city states. The most ancient of these is to be found in the remains of Çatalhöyük (Chat-al Hoo-yook), near Konya in modern Turkey. The oldest layer so far excavated

Seated Woman of Çatalhöyük
Photo by Marcus Mason at Çatalhöyük Museum, 2005

at Çatalhöyük has been carbon dated to 6500 BCE, although there may be other layers beneath this.

Many stone goddess figurines have been unearthed here, among them the 'Seated Woman of Çatalhöyük', flanked by two lions. The all-nurturing, all-providing Mother Goddess was the most potent symbol of the Cancerian Age. Cancer is ruled by the Moon, which governs the female reproductive cycle and the cycles of plant growth. The development of agriculture was dependent on understanding the natural cycles of plant growth, when to plant, when to harvest and so on. This ancient knowledge is put to effective use today in Biodynamic agriculture, working with the cycles of the Moon.

The lions on either side of the Goddess refer to her having 'tamed' the powerful, wild energy of the previous Age of Leo; in much the same way as Jesus tamed the energy of the Aries Ram, to become the 'Lamb of God'.

The taming of the lion is mirrored, centuries later, in Tarot card 8 (Strength), where the Cancer Goddess is seen gently subduing the Leo lion (see page 41).

Age of Leo

The Age of the fire sign Leo coincides with the last great Ice Age, whose sudden melting as global temperatures warmed is probably the origin of the worldwide Flood Myths – a topic too wide to explore here.

A more detailed exploration of how the Archetypes have manifested and changes have occurred in each of the previous Great Ages is beyond the scope of this book. However, the above outline should begin to give a sense of how some of the most significant shifts in global consciousness, culture and

Tarot Card 8 – Strength
Photo by Marcus Mason, 2011

technology have occurred with the changing of the Ages. A summary of the changing Ages of the last 13,000 years is given in Appendix A.

An appreciation of the scale of past changes may help us to understand the dramatic changes that are occurring in the outside world and the power of the psychological shifts that are occurring within us. It is important to realize that external events often mirror our internal confusion or resistance to change. The more we can adapt and align ourselves with these enormous global, solar and galactic energy shifts, the easier our transition is likely to be.

The Change from Pisces to Aquarius

We have seen that the changing of the Ages is a gradual process, as the Equinoctial point slowly shifts from one constellation to the next. There is no exact 'cut-off date'; rather it is a gradual shift and overlap, as the energies and archetypes of one Age give way to those of the next. As one Age dies, another Age is born, and in this process of death and rebirth there is much confusion as our psyches attempt to assimilate and integrate the huge shifts within our consciousness and even within our physical and cellular structure.

The Mayan Calendar 'end date' in December 2012 marks a crucial stage in the ongoing process of movement from the Age of Pisces into the Age of Aquarius. This date may be seen as the 'point of no return', marking the final demise of the power of the old archetypes and paradigms of the Piscean Age, many of which are desperately clinging to life.

After 2012, more and more people will awaken to the realization that the old ways no longer work; they will seem like an illusion, as if we are waking from a dream (or a nightmare!) There has already been a rude global awakening to the 'illusion' of the international banking system. It seems inevitable that more such realizations are in the offing – perhaps awakening us to the fact that governments do not know what is really happening or what to do about it.

When we perceive the chaos around us, we as rational beings can assume that there must be some 'master plan' behind it all. This is an unconscious projection born out of our own feelings of powerlessness to counteract the mindless, rumbling machine that has been unleashed. In the Book of Revelations, these are described as the 'great beasts'.

Whenever we give away our power to something greater than ourselves, we perpetuate that sense of loss of control. This applies at all levels, from the giving away of our power to parents, siblings, friends, lovers, employers, governments and even to God – the minute we project a god or goddess outside of ourselves, as separate from ourselves, then we perpetuate a sense of duality and of our own separation from the Oneness of everything. This is beautifully and succinctly expressed by Joseph Campbell in *Oriental Mythology* (p.14): 'As long as an illusion of ego remains, the commensurate illusion of a separate deity also will be there; and vice versa, as long as the idea of a separate deity is cherished, an illusion of ego, related to it in love, fear, worship, exile, or atonement, will also be there. But precisely that illusion of duality is the trick of *maya* (illusion)... In the beginning, as we have read, there was only the Self; but it said 'I'... and immediately felt fear, after which desire.'[7]

The key to overcoming this cycle of duality is to become fully conscious. Not the type of consciousness that conspiracy theorists would have us follow, by making us aware of the many ways in which we are apparently controlled by an 'elite', or by unscrupulous ETs, or by 'lizards', or by a long forgotten race of space beings (gods) who messed with our DNA, or shifted around the planets of the Solar System, which inhibited our ability to perceive things clearly. That type of 'awareness' simply leads us into greater levels of duality and feelings of helplessness and fear about the vastness of the 'problem', which is itself just a part of the 'Illusion' that we are separate.

We need to become conscious that we are co-creators of our own reality, not separate from Earth, or any of the beings who live on Her. When we understand this, then we will become truly free, no matter how chaotic, mad or senseless the world around us may appear to be.

Moving from Illusion to Wisdom

The new energetic frequencies of the Aquarian Age and the spiritual archetypes that are emerging are still very much in their embryonic stage. The Mayan calendar 'end date' represents a moment of birth of those new qualities of consciousness into our collective awareness. After that time, there is likely to be an exponential 'leap' in consciousness as more and more people begin to realize that the old limiting Archetypes and paradigms of the last 2,000 years are no longer with us, and that we can quite literally create a new world. No one is going to do this for us – this is our wake-up call to come of age and take full responsibility for our individual and collective future.

Chapter 3

AN INTRODUCTION TO ASTROLOGY

This chapter introduces astrology, outlining the psychological and spiritual meanings of the planets, to help you follow the example charts and the sequence of astrological alignments in the build-up to 2012.

The Astrology Chart

An Astrology Chart has six different layers (see Colour Plate 13). At the centre is the Earth, from where we observe the planets and stars. While we know the Earth orbits the Sun, the astrology charts depict the planets viewed from our Earth-based perspective. The circle at the centre of the chart also represents our inner spiritual core, or essence. We can only experience the true depth of this aspect of ourselves when we are fully alive, present and grounded in the Here and Now. If we are not, then we cannot hope to integrate the many subtle, refined and powerful levels of our psycho-spiritual nature, represented by the planets.

The Aspect Pattern

Around the central circle is a complex pattern of coloured lines, known as 'aspects'. These are the geometric patterns created by the positions of the planets, seen from our Earthly perspective. Many possible aspects could be used, but the most significant are those formed by 30° divisions of the circle. The conjunction (0°) is where two planets are at the same degree or within just a few degrees of each other. When more than two planets are in conjunction, this is referred to as a 'stellium'.

There is an allowable 'orb' (plus or minus up to 10°) for each aspect. The 'orbs' vary with different schools of astrological thought, but it is safe to say that the more exact an aspect, the more powerful its significance.

Red aspects (90° 'squares' and 180° 'oppositions') embody energy, tension and dynamic movement. Blue aspects (60° 'sextiles' and 120° 'trines') are concerned with harmony, substance, talents, skills and abilities. Green aspects (30° semi-sextiles and 150° quincunxes) are concerned with the development of consciousness, learning and self-awareness. For the purposes of this book, only these aspects will be considered.

Aspects create a particular dynamic between the qualities of two or more planets, affecting the way that we experience those qualities in our lives. For instance, two planets in a 'square' (90°) relationship create a tension that needs to find an outlet or resolution. This often involves dynamic action or movement in order to resolve the challenges of the 'square'. The same two planets in a 'trine' (120°) relationship would indicate a gentler, more harmonious, smoothly flowing dynamic.

The Planets

The planets represent different qualities within the human psyche. Understanding and integrating their combined effects enables us to become complete, rounded individuals. The Solar System was formed out of one original substance, gradually becoming differentiated and defined as the Sun, planets, moons, asteroids, planetoids and comets. We have evolved from that same primordial substance. It is rational to suppose that as we embody the same substances as our Solar System, we are subject to the same laws and rhythms that govern the movements and cycles of the planets around the Sun.

The human psyche is thus a microcosm of the macrocosm of the Solar System. Strictly speaking, we should include the movements of every object out there to gain a complete view of our consciousness, but this would result in information overload. In recent years, some astrologers have understood the importance and significance of the asteroids; the four brightest are included in this book.

The Sun (Helios) ⊙

The Sun is the source of light, energy and life in our Solar System and represents these qualities in the human psyche. It shows our fundamental nature, how we 'shine' out in the world. As we learn to refine the qualities of our Sun sign, this gradually shifts our identification with our ego, to reveal our true spiritual identity.

In many ancient traditions, the Sun corresponds with the Heart, as the source of life. When we lose connection with our heart, then we tend to express the more negative, neurotic or selfish qualities of our Sun sign. Realigning fully with our heart, we express its more compassionate, loving and selfless qualities.

The Sun 'rules' the zodiac sign of Leo, also associated with the Heart. Ancient cultures understood that sunlight is the medium through which the Life-force is carried: it is the *Qi (Ch'i)* energy of Chinese Medicine, Taoism and Martial Arts (Qi Gong, T'ai Ch'i, etc); it is the *Prana* of Indian Yoga, the *Etheric Energy* of Theosophy, etc. Even our material-based culture recognizes that sunlight affects the Life-force in plants, through photosynthesis.

As we breathe, we take in air imbued with Life-force, carried in sunlight. This goes from our lungs into the blood and is carried to the heart and circulation. From here, our blood circulates to literally carry the life-giving energy of sunlight into every cell of our bodies.

The ancient Chinese sages described the *'Shen'* – our individual spiritual spark, created from the One Source, or *Tao*. *'Shen'* is the quality of our spirit that 'dwells' in the heart. If the heart is poorly nourished with de-vitalized food, negative thoughts or feelings, then our Spirit becomes agitated and cannot settle happily in the body; we cannot fully incarnate, and will exhibit the more challenging, negative qualities of our Sun sign. If the heart is well nourished with good food, positive thoughts and feelings, our Spirit will be healthy, happy filled with energy, joy and love, and the heart will thrive.

Mercury (Hermes) ☿

Mercury whizzes around the Sun every 88 days. It is dynamic, fast-moving and fluid, distributing and communicating raw solar energy and consciousness to the rest of the Solar System. In the human psyche, Mercury represents all forms of communication and connections between people and systems; it governs intelligence, speech, listening and the discerning faculties of the mind.

Mercury expresses itself through logical, rational thinking in Air signs (Gemini, Libra, Aquarius), practical, pragmatic thinking in Earth signs (Taurus, Virgo, Capricorn), emotional, empathic intelligence in Water signs (Cancer, Scorpio, Pisces) and intuitive, inspirational intelligence in Fire signs (Aries, Leo, Sagittarius).

All intelligence types are equally valid; however, someone with an Air-sign Mercury may be hard pushed to see the logic of someone with a Water-sign Mercury, and vice versa! If the different types of intelligence and their corresponding needs were properly understood and valued by educational systems, there would be fewer people suffering from a lack of self-belief in their intelligence or abilities.

Mercury weaves together many threads of consciousness in order to form opinions, make decisions, and communicate. Mercury is the messenger of the gods, reaching up to grasp the most exalted levels of consciousness, then swooping down on winged sandals to give attention to the smallest details.

Sometimes Mercury can find it hard to discern the relative value of what is perceived and fail to grasp that because something is possible, it is not necessarily desirable, appropriate or in the interests of the greater whole. There are many examples of so-called 'rational' thinking resulting in disaster, because the bigger picture was ignored. It is important for Mercury to listen to the larger (common sense) view and vision of Jupiter, to prevent such mistakes from happening.

Venus (Aphrodite) ♀

Venus is a planet of contrasts. Viewed from Earth, her light is the most beautiful of all the planets. This beauty is created by sunlight, reflected by her sulphuric acid cloud cover; on the surface below a violent furnace constantly rages. Venus' outward beauty, radiance and grace are born from the intense, creative and transformative fires of love within.

The mythological story of Venus' birth sheds light on what lies behind her more superficial qualities. Ouranus (Heaven) was the husband of Gaia (Earth); they had many children, among them Kronos (Saturn). The patriarchal myths of classical Greece and Rome tell how Ouranus was so repulsed by his children, his physical creations, that he confined them to Tartarus, the realm of Hades (Pluto). The spiritual qualities that his creations embodied became entrapped in the material world and unable to commune with Spirit, creating a separation between Spirit and matter.

Because of this spiritual tyranny, Gaia then incited Kronos (Saturn) to overpower Ouranus; Gaia and Kronos (Saturn) both represent more physical expressions of the Spirit. Kronos castrated Ouranus, hurling his testicles into the sea, which represents the descent of the creative power of the Spirit into the unconscious realm of the feelings. Venus was born from the surging foam that resulted, bringing the redemptive quality of Love to reunite Heaven and Earth within us.

This redemptive Love manifests in different forms; sexual love (Eros) is a means of experiencing ecstatic union with another human, and potentially with the Divine; platonic love (Philos), or friendship enables the expression of unselfishness and altruism; the transcendent and selfless love of the Spirit (Agape) enables self-forgetting and the potential to move beyond ego boundaries (Saturn) and reunite with the Spirit within.

Each of these paths of Love holds an enticing goal. To reach the goal, we are tested in the fires of Love – not to prove our worthiness to any Divine Being 'out there', but to develop the inner qualities, emotional strengths and spiritual integrity that will enable us to surrender our ego-self and integrate the piercing light of enlightenment.

The Moon (Artemis/Selene) ☽

Earth and Moon are intimately linked, with a common centre of gravity, as if connected by an invisible umbilical cord. The Moon is just 240,250 miles from Earth and has a profound energetic and physical effect on all of the fluids and consciousness here on Earth.

The Moon reflects our feelings, in all their moods. It represents the energetic core of our Emotional (Astral) body, enabling us to perceive the world and respond to it through our feelings. The Moon controls rhythms, cycles of growth and the movements of subtle energies. It affects the movements of all of the fluids in the body, including the cerebro-spinal fluid, which surrounds the brain and central nervous system.

The Moon 'weaves' an energetic 'web' around the Earth, affecting the flow of energy in our bodies and in the energy-pathways of our planet. Acupuncture describes subtle energy pathways, or 'meridians' in the human body, and there are similar energy pathways in the Earth. In the human, the Qi energy resides deep within the organs – heart, liver, spleen, lungs, kidneys etc – then rises to the surface, flowing along the 'meridians' creating vortices at the acupuncture 'points'.

Similarly, there are great 'Dragon Lines' encircling the Earth, forming powerful and often complex energy vortices at sacred sites – the equivalent of acupuncture points on the Earth. There are also thousands of minor energy lines.

The Moon's monthly cycle around the Earth affects all of these, and we in turn are affected by these rhythms. The Moon continually 'filters' the energetic influences from the other planets, creating complex relationships and distributing their frequencies into the grid structures of the Earth and through them, into us.

We receive these resonances and frequencies primarily through our feet, which is why it is important to be properly grounded in order to find emotional balance. The more sensitive our feelings, the more keenly we will feel these effects and influences from the Moon. If we are cut off from our feelings, living only from the level of the mind, then this may seem to be nonsense; there is no other way to experience the reality of these subtle energies and influences except through our feeling senses. This is why attempts at making machines to accurately measure subtle energies fail; the best 'instruments' for verifying this are not machines, but finely honed and reliable feeling perceptions.

The Moon's Nodes

The Moon's Nodes are concerned with our Spiritual Destiny or inner Life Purpose.

The Moon's Nodes form an axis, where the plane of the Moon's orbit around the Earth intersects with the plane of the Ecliptic – Earth's orbit around the Sun:

The North (Ascending) and South (Descending) Nodes define our line of karma and destiny. They work together as

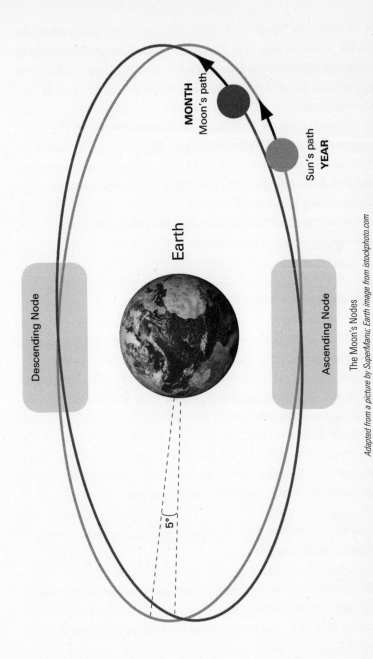

MONTH
Moon's path

Sun's path
YEAR

Earth

Descending Node

Ascending Node

5°

The Moon's Nodes

Adapted from a picture by SuperManu; Earth image from istockphoto.com

a polarity; the South Node relates to the past – our past lives, karma, and our past evolutionary experiences; the North Node indicates the qualities that we need to cultivate to follow our spiritual path for this lifetime, and move forward to new levels of awareness.

The Nodes are the energetic points that bring the Sun, Moon and Earth – Spirit, Soul and Body – into relationship. The Nodal axis indicates the fine line that we need to tread in order to fulfil our spiritual, psychological and physical destiny. By resolving past karma, we can draw on the best qualities of our past, which act as the fuel that propels us toward our true spiritual purpose for this lifetime.

Moon's South Node ☋

The South Node indicates our spiritual past, the path trodden in previous lives, which has led to our present state of evolution. This is why, in our early years, we may mistake what has served us in the past as being our spiritual path in this lifetime, as we unconsciously recognize the spiritual teachings, or indeed teachers, from our past. So, the first lesson is to let go of our attachments to the ideas, beliefs and people who may have guided us in the past, and then focus our spiritual attention in the direction where the North Node now lies.

Moon's North Node ☊

The North Node is the most important indicator of the soul's purpose, in the astrological chart. Its meaning is often very subtle, and may only really be understood at the deepest levels of one's being, after much life experience... only you can really know what your North Node is about.

The position of the North Node indicates the soul qualities that need to be cultivated in order to follow our true path. It is important to develop the most refined, spiritual qualities of the North Node's zodiac position, in order to move forward, heal, and release the deeper qualities of the sign position of the South Node. The North Node holds the key to how to heal our inner wounds from the past, those patterns that keep us in a state of separation.

Mars (Ares) ♂

Mars represents outgoing, creative energy, manifesting as will, drive, power, ambition, and sexuality. It is the drive to explore and go beyond our immediate experience and familiar surroundings; the energy of motivation and movement that acts to create change. Mars is highly motivated, focused, direct and incisive, bringing qualities of endurance, discernment, courage, strength and integrity, but can also be forceful, ambitious, relentless, even brutal.

Mars can become highly skilled, honing its creativity to peak performance. Mars' main challenge is to express itself non-violently, to become the 'spiritual warrior', understanding the Taoist ideal of 'non-action' (*wu wei*), or action flowing effortlessly from our spiritual core – the opposite of the forced enactment of the ego's desires.

We need Mars' energy to act in the world, to manifest our thoughts, feelings and will. The key to its creative use is not to identify with the will, but to understand that its creative power flows through us from our Spirit. This connection with Will makes Mars more prone than other planets to become caught in the ego's rapture and to lose our sense of objectivity or detachment.

When Mars serves the interests of the ego, there is always the danger of it becoming destructive. When it serves our inner spiritual will (Pluto) then it can accomplish great things, calling on inner resources of endurance, strength and courage, to fulfil our noblest aspirations. Mars' ability to act well depends on our capacity for commitment to a goal or ideal, greater than the narrow interests of our ego self.

The 'Asteroid Goddesses'

The Asteroid Belt lies between the orbits of the inner, rocky planets and the outer 'gas giants'. The four asteroids described below were the first and brightest to be discovered. They represent qualities of the soul, which act as a bridge between the personality (inner planets) and the Spirit (outer planets).

Ceres (Demeter) ♀

Ceres is the largest and only spherical body in the Asteroid Belt; it is classified as a 'Dwarf Planet'.

Ceres represents the Mother Goddess, how we relate to Earth as a sentient being, and our attitudes toward nurturing others and ourselves. She reveals qualities of the positive inner Mother, which may reflect or contrast with our actual experience of our physical mother.

Ceres holds the key to healing any wounds of childhood, arising from our relationship with our mother. Often, the way we care for others can be at our own expense, particularly if we did not receive good emotional nurture as children. Ceres shows what is needed to nurture ourselves; when we become filled, this can then extend out to nurture others.

Ceres' nurturing energy is drawn from the Earth and focused at the 'Hara' energy centre at the navel. When we learn to cultivate this centre through spiritual practice such as T'ai Ch'i, Qi Gong or Yoga, the Hara becomes our energetic umbilical cord to Mother Earth.

Pallas Athene (Athena) ⚛

Pallas Athene is our inner female warrior, selflessly fighting for truth, justice and protecting the integrity of our hearts. In her essence, Pallas expresses a creative mind, linked to a strong heart; if expressed negatively, this may lead to fanaticism.

Pallas' approach is defensive, her goal to maintain order, based on inner values. She has had a tendency to become detached from the body and feelings, but this has been changing since her triple alignment with Pluto in 2001. In mythology, Athena sprang fully armoured from the brow of Zeus (Jupiter). She represents creative feminine power, equal to Zeus' masculine power. She instigates change, particularly when a situation becomes dangerously imbalanced. Her interventions are clear, decisive, uncompromising and effective.

Pallas often provides the motivation behind the actions of Mars, the male hero or warrior. It was Athena who sent Perseus to slay the Gorgon. Perseus, the hero, acted on her behalf, while she provided him with wisdom, strategy and magic to achieve her goals.

She is uncompromising in showing us where our boundaries need to be to maintain order and integrity, keeping our heart safe and protected from unwanted influences and the distractions of our ego.

Vesta (Hestia) ⚶

Vesta connects with our inner heart's spiritual essence. She is inwardly focused, still, self-contained and deeply aligned with the creative 'Kundalini' energy, underlying our sexuality, creativity and soul's ability to express itself through the heart.

Vesta expresses that aspect of the feminine, which has no need for relationship. While she may choose to enter into relationship, she retains her integrity and independence, remaining mistress of her fate. Vesta's 'virginity' describes this ability to remain whole while in relationship. She is able to give freely of herself, without giving herself away to another. Vesta teaches us how to integrate our sexuality with our spirituality.

Vesta combines a subtle vulnerability with the constantly self-renewing power of the creative force. This enables the expression of intimacy, emotional honesty and integrity; she is reliant on the qualities of Pallas Athene and Mars to protect her vulnerability.

Juno (Hera) ⚵

Juno represents the principle of committed relationship, marriage and the search for a soul partner. She reminds us of the 'soul contracts' that need to be fulfilled during our lifetime. She carries our soul's memory of past lifetimes, and intuits what is needed for us to bring about the 'inner marriage' of the male and female aspects of our psyche.

In mythology, Juno was married to Jupiter, holding her marriage as a sacred union. Jupiter, on the other hand, seemed to thrive on infidelity and promiscuity with many different goddesses, humans, nymphs and so on. This dynamic created a pattern where Juno became the archetype of the abused partner, fuelled by her fidelity to an unfaithful partner, adhering to an ideal even though the reality was far from that. Juno can see right into the soul of another, so it can be difficult for her to separate the beauty of another's soul from the unacceptable or unintegrated behaviour of their personality.

Juno, however, can help us to recognize these patterns, which are often inherited from parents and grandparents, so that we can rediscover our true inner worth and create relationships based on equality, trust, integrity and honest communication at all levels. The need to create 'Right Relations' is what underlies all of our past-life karma, and the 'soul contracts' that we undertake in this life in order to redress the imbalances of the past.

Jupiter (Zeus) ♃

Jupiter is the largest planet in the Solar System. It represents the creative power of the imagination to envision new levels of being and bring them into manifestation.

Jupiter has a dual movement of energy, being both active and receptive. It represents the urge to extend our horizons, perceptions and possibilities. In doing so, it creates space to receive previously unimagined insights, visions and creative potentials. Our willingness to create this inner psychological space allows the New to flow into us. The more we can imagine, the more possibilities open up for us.

Jupiter connects us with levels of awareness beyond the rational, defining how we perceive reality through our senses, intuition, imagination and observation. Jupiter enables us to build a complete picture of the world around us; this whole perception allows us to test the reality of our insights in the real world.

As always, the physical planet manifests its spiritual qualities. Jupiter has a vast atmosphere, forming the bulk of its body. The pressure in the depths of its atmosphere is such that the gases of the upper atmosphere become transformed into liquefied metallic hydrogen, around its relatively small core. This reminds us of strength and resilience needed to anchor our dreams into reality. If we get carried away with endless possibilities, then we remain forever in a state of 'the grass being always greener', without manifesting the Vision of how our life could be. Jupiter's extreme internal pressures remind us of the focus required to marry our dreams with what is possible, and to remain aligned with the reality of the greater Whole. We need always to test our dreams and perceptions against reality, which is the realm of Saturn.

Saturn (Kronos) ♄

Saturn is the last planet visible to the naked eye and represents physical boundaries and limitations. Saturn is the great form giver, challenging us to incarnate our soul's full potentials. In doing this, it reveals our limitations, fears and the repressed 'Shadow'[1] within our unconscious, enabling us to confront it, unlock its creative potentials and move beyond the known and familiar.

Saturn tests the structures we create in our lives; physical structures concerned with our home, work and creativity;

emotional structures of relationships; mental structures, concepts and beliefs that we create in order to relate to the spiritual. Periodically Saturn tests whether these structures are strong and flexible enough to contain the powerful energies of our Spirit, represented by the outer planets, Uranus, Neptune and Pluto.

If the structures are strong and based in reality, they will support us, enabling us to manifest our fullest potentials; if they are not, we will need to create better, stronger and more appropriate structures to manifest our potentials.

For these challenging times, a new helper and guide for our journey into the beyond was discovered in 1977 – the enigmatic planetoid Chiron, orbiting in between Saturn and Uranus.

Chiron ⚷

Chiron represents the inner healer and shaman, revealing where we experience our sense of spiritual wounding, loss or separation and holding the keys to reconnect us with our spiritual Source.

Chiron is a shape-shifter; its highly elliptical orbit extends from just inside Saturn's orbit, out to Uranus. Initially it was unclear whether Chiron was an asteroid or a comet and then in 1989, as it approached closer to the Sun, it developed a comet-like tail. It is now considered to have a dual identity.

Like the shamans of old, Chiron is an enigma and a maverick, moving between the physical realm (Saturn) and the spiritual realms (Uranus). This can make him seem threatening to the established order; yet, there is an eternal fascination with his insight, healing abilities and the spiritual gifts that he brings into our lives.

In Greek mythology, Chiron was the wisest of the Centaurs, renowned as a warrior and teacher of astrology, healing, hunting, music and gymnastics. He was able to pull forth information and wisdom from the Cosmos (Uranus) and apply it to any number of practical ends (Saturn).

Chiron uses the transformative energies of Spirit for healing the body, emotions and mind. He needs to remain free from material attachments to work with the realities of the spirit and its expression through the Life-force.

The discovery of Chiron in 1977 coincided with a growing awareness and acceptance of many forms of energy-medicine and spiritual practices, such as Spiritual Healing, Acupuncture, Crystal Healing, Homoeopathy, Bach Flower remedies, Yoga, T'ai Ch'i and Aikido.

Chiron reminds us of our instinctual knowing of the innate relationship between matter and spirit, and that the Life-force flows through all living things. Chiron's true healing potential is to reconnect us to the Oneness of all Life, something that was understood by ancient cultures throughout the world.

Uranus (Ouranos) ♅

Uranus breaks all the 'rules' of planetary rotation. Lying on its back, tilted at an angle of 98°, alternately presenting its poles and equator toward the Sun as it orbits, it rotates on its axis in the opposite direction to most other planets, except Venus. Uranus' magnetic field is tilted at an angle of about 60° to its rotational plane. It is believed that these eccentricities may be the result of a violent collision long ago.

Uranus awakens us to other dimensions, by helping to break through the structures we have created that do not allow the full awareness or expression of our true nature. It brings insight, illumination and wisdom in ways that are unexpected, exciting, energizing and sometimes shocking.

Uranus shows us how to express our individual genius, the unique quality of being that we bring to Life. We all possess this as a potential and many factors determine how far we can realize it. Above all, we need to break free from our conditioning, security patterns, comfort zones, fears, inhibitions, stuck emotional and mental patterns, so that we may live more fully in the moment.

Uranus can challenge and inspire us when we learn to integrate its high frequencies, and approach life from the spiritual perspective of wisdom, detachment, intuition and inner knowing.

Neptune (Poseidon) Ψ

Neptune opens our hearts to Unconditional Love, and our connection with Infinite Being, through the processes of surrender, forgiveness and devotion to something greater than our ego selves.

Whereas Uranus breaks through our resistances and ego structures, Neptune dissolves the boundaries of the ego, enabling us to absorb spiritual energies and qualities, particularly Love. Loving surrender enables us to merge with the formlessness of Being.

Neptune has a reputation for vagueness, but this only occurs when its energies overwhelm the personality structures and are not integrated. Because of its transcendental qualities, Neptune can also lead to many forms of escapism, if we are unwilling to allow the process of surrender that true spiritual growth requires. Hence Neptune's influence may also create delusions, escapism into drink, drugs, fantasy, ungrounded idealism or beliefs, attachments to cults or personalities, fanaticism, addictions of many kinds – in fact, anything involving a search for escape.

Far from being concerned just with escapism, Neptune strips away our ego's Illusion of separation from Oneness; it dis-illusions us about the glamours offered by escapism, and helps us merge our consciousness into the greater spiritual reality, whose essence is pure Unconditional Love. In this way, Neptune opens us to direct felt experience of the Divine within, bringing inspiration, experience of blissful transcendence, joy and the knowing that we are One with All that Is.

Pluto (Hades) ♇

In August 2006, Pluto was reclassified by the IAU (International Astronomical Union), as a 'Dwarf Planet'. It should be made clear that this classification is solely for the convenience of astronomers, and has little to do with the energetic qualities of this powerful and potent object, whose discovery in 1930 triggered the Nuclear Age and a collective awakening to the true power of the Unconscious.

Pluto may be small and remote, but its energetic effects are like those of a high potency homoeopathic remedy, which can be deep acting, bringing about inner transformation at a profound level. You can be assured that Pluto is not aware of having been 'demoted', as we observe its effects in our lives!

We have seen how Neptune strips away the Illusion of separation, and the glamour of escapism, enabling us to merge with the greater Reality, whose essence is Unconditional Love.

In order to reach this state and remain in it, we need Pluto to reveal the unresolved aspects of our Shadow. These are the parts of us that unconsciously deny our true spiritual will, and undermine our ability to remain consciously aware of our Oneness. This process can be very disruptive to our ego structures, and the unconscious contents released may sometimes feel threatening and destructive. However, Pluto's underlying purpose is always to bring us to a greater understanding and acceptance of the power of our inner spiritual light and spiritual Will to Be.

Pluto embodies our true will and the unlimited power that it holds, so every time we consciously or unconsciously deny it or allow it to be denied by others, this powerful creative force is pushed into our unconscious. It may then become self-destructive, or be projected out onto others, who are seen to manifest the powerful qualities that we have suppressed or denied. Such projection sometimes takes the form of giving spiritual power away to another because we do not feel capable or responsible enough to wield it; in this case we will tend to look up to that person, or what they represent. Alternatively, we may perceive our projected power as entirely negative, believing that we are being controlled, manipulated or in the grip of some conspiracy against us.

Thus the radiant power of our spiritual will becomes projected onto leaders, teachers, parents, politicians, bosses, religious leaders, icons, gurus, celebrities, in fact anyone to whom we attribute those deep qualities of spirituality, power, control, or tyranny that we may deny, or fear in ourselves. When we engage in a power struggle with one of these beings (and so confronting our own inner demons), it heralds the beginning of the process of reclaiming those unconscious contents, and regaining our inner power. This process enables us to transmute our apparent darkness back into Light.

Pluto reveals the true power and potential of our spiritual nature and the boundless possibilities open to us when we fully own this aspect of ourselves.

The New 'Planetoids' or 'Trans-Neptunian Objects'

Since 1998, many small planetoids are being discovered beyond Pluto, some in the Kuiper Belt and some in the Oort Cloud beyond. These bodies are variously referred to as Planetoids, Plutoids, Trans-Neptunian Objects (TNO), Kuiper Belt Objects (KBO), Cubewanos and Dwarf Planets.

Whatever their official name and classification, it has been agreed to name them after gods and goddesses of the Underworld, from different creation myths. As each 'new' one appears, it further defines and differentiates the many-faceted qualities of the Collective Unconscious, which were previously all lumped together under the 'Death, Regeneration and Rebirth' auspices of Pluto.

As we extend our awareness beyond the planets of the outer Solar System, we move into the area of unresolved, hidden agendas lurking within the human psyche. These aspects of the collective Shadow have been subtly undermining our spiritual progress for thousands of years. The more layers of unconscious material that come to light, the more fully awake we can all ultimately become.

The timing of these discoveries is significant, nearly all following the 1999 conjunction of Chiron and Pluto on 30 December. This heralded the beginning of a deep Healing of these long-unconscious energies and archetypes, and of a return to our connection with our Spiritual Source.

The significance of these Trans-Neptunian objects increased as Pluto aligned with the Galactic Centre in 2007, helping to bring their qualities more fully into awareness. This is not an easy process, as they challenge us to confront hidden or obscure aspects of our Collective Shadow. At the heart of these dark and apparently destructive qualities lie the clues to understanding why and where we feel separate from the Light. These archetypes have resulted from the collective denial of our Inner Light, over millennia.

Each new discovery brings the opportunity to reclaim hidden aspects of the Collective Unconscious. We ignore them at our peril. These extremely powerful forces, which have been ignored for so long, wreak havoc when we deny their presence, or reject the qualities they represent. Ignoring them fuels their more negative aspects; we cannot afford to resist engaging with these emerging aspects of Being.

These new discoveries, and their meanings, are explored in the next chapter.

The Tropical Zodiac Signs

Beyond the planets, the next layer out shows the Tropical Zodiac signs, with each planet positioned in one of the signs. The zodiac signs represent ancestral, archetypal qualities, carrying within them the accumulated experiences of our evolutionary journey on Earth. They connect us to the four 'Elements', Fire, Earth, Air and Water. These help to define our temperament, colouring and qualifying the ways that we experience the planets.

The 'Elements' represent the energetic qualities that manifest as the physical elements – the 'Etheric forces', as they have been called – the understanding of which became corrupted in mediaeval times as the four 'humours'. In Chinese medicine and philosophy, they are known as the changing phases of Qi (life-force) energy.

The Four Elements form a creative cycle around the zodiac wheel, each giving rise to the next element. They are explored more fully in later chapters.

See Appendix B for a summary of the planets and zodiac signs, their glyphs and meanings.

The Astrological Houses

The Houses are the 'cake-like' segments where the planets are found, representing different areas of life and the environment

The Astrological Houses

into which we are born. The houses orient us in Time and Space, through the East–West Horizon and the North–South Meridian.

The planets' positions in the houses are defined by location (and time of birth, or of a particular event). So, for the purposes of this book, we will not focus on the houses, as the planetary alignments will affect people at all locations around the globe.

The Sidereal Zodiac of 'Fixed' Stars

The final, outermost layer of the chart shows the positions of the constellations, or Sidereal Zodiac, and many of the brightest stars. These are known as the 'fixed stars' because, relative to the planets, they appear static. They move slowly due to Precession, and of course have their own movement through Space, but the stars lie at such vast distances from Earth that their movements appear almost imperceptible. This is why the patterns of the constellations have remained the same for thousands for years.

Chapter 4
THE APPROACH TO 2012 (1999–2005)

If we look at the major astrological alignments that have occurred in recent years, this will help us to understand the changes that 2012 brings. A pivotal point in preparing our consciousness for the deep changes that we are now experiencing was the Total Solar Eclipse of August 1999.

We have already seen that the shift between ages is a long process, spanning decades. Profound changes never hinge on just one event; they proceed in a series of steps, each preparing us to receive and integrate the next. If we fail to integrate any of these steps, this makes the next one more challenging. If we are in denial that a significant change is occurring, we may simply feel confused and see the world as a random, chaotic place. Nothing could be further from the truth; what follows illustrates the impeccable Cosmic Order unfolding around us.

Many people are currently struggling to keep pace with the changing energies. Although the alignments below have passed, seeing them in sequence may help us to understand what has already happened and what is yet to come. The more we approach these changes with an open heart, a clear mind and inner balance, the easier and more positive it will be for us.

Total Solar Eclipse (11 August 1999)

This Eclipse, close to the end of the last millennium, captured the imaginations of millions. The Eclipse shadow began its journey south of Nova Scotia and swept across the North Atlantic, over Europe, the Middle East and India (see diagram on page 73).

Solar Eclipses have a profound effect on the Earth's subtle energy grids and ley lines. All powerful events that occur on Earth leave energetic memory imprints in the Earth's subtle energy. These can become amplified and perpetuated by the energy flow through the grids, which is fed by the movements of the Sun, Moon and planets. Powerful negative imprints, such as war or emotional trauma, can block the energy flow in a particular part of the planet, causing it to stagnate.

An eclipse provides an opportunity to release both positive and negative energetic imprints. The renowned dowser, Hamish Miller[1] found that, as an eclipse shadow passes overhead, the Earth's subtle energy lines power down to almost nothing, becoming indiscernible to dowsing; then as the light returns, the grids spring back into life. This is a bit like deleting old software and loading new software into a computer, then rebooting the system.

During the 1999 Eclipse, the cosmic dance of planets above the sacred places of the Earth played out like a beautifully orchestrated symphony. The full scenario would require too much space here, but suffice to say that at each major transition during this event, planets were aligned directly above many of the world's most important sacred sites. A brief précis of these transitions is given below.

As an eclipse shadow passes over the Earth from west to east, so do the north–south meridians[2] of the Sun, Moon and planets progress from east to west. While the eclipse shadow

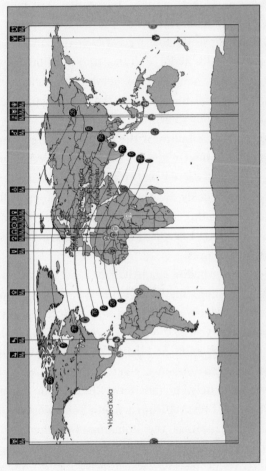

August 1999 Eclipse Path and planetary 'Meridians' at Maximum Eclipse (11:08 UT/GMT)

releases old energy 'imprints', the north–south meridians of the planets will at the same time become aligned over sacred sites, which can enable new patterns to be created, particularly when people gather at these sites for prayer, meditation or sacred ceremony. This amplifies the creative possibilities for 'anchoring' new planetary qualities into the Earth.

The 1999 Eclipse shadow passed over the lands that had produced the world's major cultures and religions over the last 6,000 years. It heralded the demise of archetypes and paradigms, which had underpinned the cultures produced by the three Great Ages of Taurus, Aries and Pisces.

In the first few minutes of the eclipse, the meridian lines of the Moon and Sun were aligned over Mecca, Bethlehem and Jerusalem, the most sacred places of Islam, Christianity and Judaism. Simultaneously Neptune's meridian aligned directly over Hawaii, indicating a shift in Universal Consciousness toward Unconditional Love. Hawaii is one of the Earth's most powerful energy centres.

As the eclipse shadow made its first landfall over the Isles of Scilly, King Arthur's mythical 'Lyonesse', which lies off the coast of Cornwall, Uranus' meridian was aligned over Hawaii, indicating a collective awakening for humanity as a whole. The shadow then passed over St Michael's Mount, into northern France and southern Germany. Over Austria, it passed above the mysterious Teufelstein (Lucifer's Rock), with its ancient calendar of Venus. Crossing Hungary into Romania, the shadow passed over Sarmizegetusa, the 'Romanian Stonehenge', before reaching maximum eclipse near Râmnicu Vâlcea, at the exact moment when Venus' meridian was directly above, bringing the energy of Love to Earth.

As it crossed the Black Sea and over Turkey, a 90 per cent shadow passed above the Neolithic and Chalcolithitic settlement at Çatalhöyük, priming it for the release of ancient patterns that had taken root there during the Age of Cancer (see Chapter 2). (This release would complete during the Solar Eclipse of March 2006, when the path of totality passed directly over Çatalhöyük.)

The 1999 Eclipse shadow then crossed Iraq, near the Tigris and Euphrates, home to many important Biblical sites; then over Iran, birthplace of ancient Persia and Zoroastrianism; over India, birthplace of many religions including Hinduism, Buddhism and Sikhism.

The 'Mobile Planetary 6th Chakra'

Robert Coon refers to the existence of what he calls the 'Mobile Planetary 6th Chakra', the energy Centre, which holds the emerging consciousness for each New Age (Aeon)[3]. He describes how as one Aeon changes over to the next, the energetic focus for the New Aeon moves approximately 30° to the west.

At the beginning of the Age of Pisces the focus for the 6th Chakra was centred on Jerusalem and became activated at the crucifixion of Jesus. Jesus embodied the spirit of the Cosmic Christ, the creative aspect of the Divine, described as the 'Son of God'. We have seen how, in the Chinese understanding of energy, the Spirit (*Shen*) resides in the blood. So, as Jesus' blood flowed onto the Earth, the Earth became infused with the Christ Spirit; it was a marriage of Heaven and Earth. This was aided by the presence of Mother Mary, her sister Mary of Cleophas, and Mary Magdalene, at the foot of the cross. These three embodiments of aspects of the Divine Feminine were the 'midwives' who birthed this profound union of Heaven and Earth. It was the Earth herself that became the long-sought

Holy Grail, the vessel that carries the blood of Christ. (It is also true that the three Marys became carriers of the Grail at that moment.)[4]

After the Crucifixion it is believed that Jesus' uncle, Joseph of Arimathea, travelled with Mary, and probably Mary Magdalene at least as far as France, to Glastonbury where they planted the seeds to prepare Glastonbury and surrounding sites, such as Stonehenge and Avebury, to become receptacles for the (then) future energies of the Age of Aquarius.

One effect of the 1999 Eclipse was to complete the shift of focus to Glastonbury; what happened during the last 20 minutes of the eclipse reveals the intricate process of anchoring in these new Aquarian energies.

Twenty minutes before the eclipse ended, the Sun's Meridian aligned over Glastonbury and the Moon's Meridian over Stonehenge and Avebury. At the exact moment when the eclipse ended, the Sun's meridian was aligned over the Hill of Uisneach, the ancient spiritual centre of Ireland, and the Moon's meridian over Tara, the seat of the ancient kings of Ireland, also an ancient centre to the Sun Goddess, Grainne.

During this last phase of the eclipse, the new Aquarian Age archetypes were 'imprinted' on these sites in England and Ireland. The male (yang) polarity anchored into the triangle between Stonehenge, Avebury and Glastonbury, each holding a different aspect of this new consciousness. The female (yin) polarity anchored into Ireland at Tara, Uisneach and the sites of Newgrange, Knowth and Dowth in the Boyne Valley.

Crucial to this process was the 10-year dowsing journey of Hamish and Ba Miller, with Paul Broadhurst and Vivienne Shanley[5]. They followed the energies of the 'Apollo–Athene' dragon line, from Ireland, across Europe to Israel, completing this just a few months before August 1999. Their work opened the energy pathways in the Earth, enabling the shift of energies from the Middle East to Britain and Ireland. How elegantly do the paths of planetary light-workers weave their web, often unaware of the full significance of their work.

Further understanding of the 1999 Eclipse comes from looking at its astrology. Colour Plate 13 shows the geocentric (Earth-centred) chart for maximum eclipse over Romania. The big red square, or 'Grand Cross', shows the tensions and challenges needed to release the old patriarchal patterns and archetypes, and the destruction caused by the imbalanced expression of the male warrior. It brought the challenge for everyone to stand in the true power of their spiritual identity and apply that in service to the Earth.

Colour Plate 14 shows the heliocentric (Sun-centred) chart, forming a perfect six-pointed star. This indicated profound levels of spiritual Grace becoming freely available, if we could resolve the tensions of the geocentric (personality) chart, by surrendering our egos and embracing the full expression of our spiritual selves in every aspect of our lives. Collectively, we have been endeavouring to integrate these frequencies of Grace into our day-to-day consciousness ever since.

Winter Solstice Galactic Alignment
(22 December 1999, 07:44 UT)

Following the release of old archetypes at the eclipse, the first seeds of global spiritual rebirth were planted at the Winter Solstice of 1999.

This solstice marked the exact turning point in the Great Cycle of our Solar System and the Galaxy, as the Solstice Sun reached the mid-point of the Galactic Equator. This was Earth's true Galactic Solstice, the deepest point in the cycle, after which the Light then began to return.

Just as it takes three to four days for the light to return after our annual Winter Solstice (the return of the Christ-Light at Christmas), it would take another 13 years for the Galactic Light to re-emerge into our consciousness on 21 December 2012. (Fundamental numbers in the calculation of the Mayan Long Count Calendar are 13 and 20.)

The sequence of star charts on the following pages illustrates the progress of the December Solstice Sun across the Galactic Equator (GE) between 1980 and 2016.

Chiron–Pluto Conjunction (30 December 1999)

The next step in this unfolding awakening occurred with the conjunction of Chiron and Pluto on 30 December 1999. This rare alignment last occurred on 19 July 1941, the day when Winston Churchill launched the 'V for Victory' campaign across Europe. In 1941 Chiron had not been discovered, so would have been functioning mostly unconsciously.

Chiron's 1999 alignment with Pluto began the long process of healing our connection with our spiritual will. This is a powerful, creative force that enables us to create meaningful change when small individual actions are performed with full awareness and focused spiritual intent – Pluto is small, but powerful.

Two days later, on 1 January 2000 we witnessed this transformative healing power being played out globally, as we watched inspiring, moving and beautiful ceremonies unfolding peacefully, as dawn broke in each country around the world.

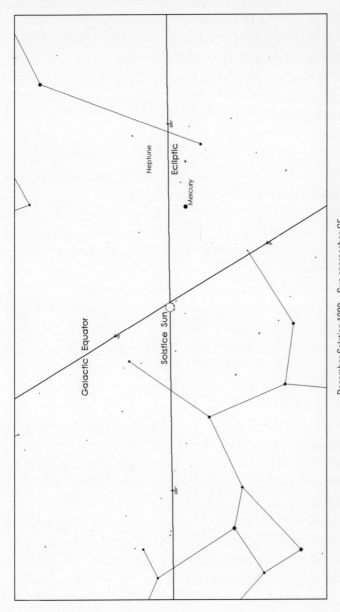

December Solstice 1980 – Sun approaches GE
Image Produced by Chris Marriott's SkyMap Pro

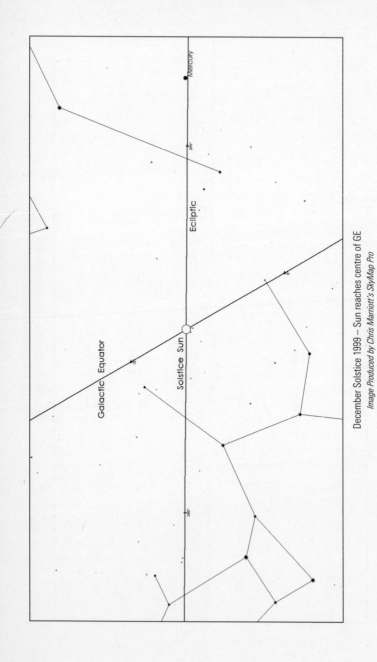

December Solstice 1999 – Sun reaches centre of GE

Image Produced by Chris Marriott's SkyMap Pro

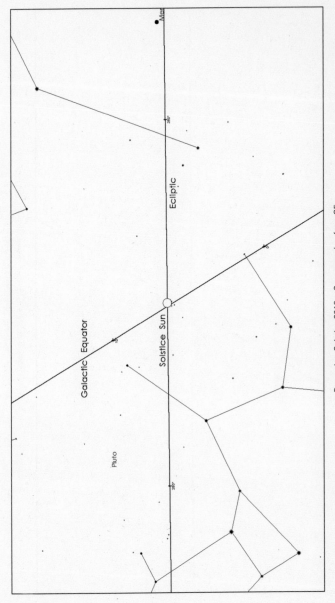

December Solstice 2012 – Sun emerging from GE
Image Produced by Chris Marriott's SkyMap Pro

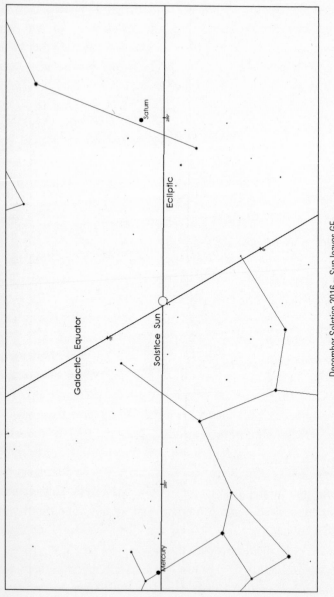

December Solstice 2016 – Sun leaves GE
Image Produced by Chris Marriott's SkyMap Pro

Since the beginning of the Millennium there have been many significant alignments and eclipses, which have all contributed to the unfolding and awakening of the new consciousness. To explore them all would require another book, so we will just consider the most significant ones between 2000 and 2005.

Alignments 2000

From 3 to 5 May 2000, a major conjunction, or Stellium, of all seven 'personal' planets (Moon, Venus, Mercury, Sun, Jupiter, Saturn and Mars) was aligned in Taurus. (Taurus is associated with the first stages of growth after a new beginning.) This rare alignment, nine months after the 1999 Eclipse, enabled us to begin manifesting the new energies, archetypes and potentials that were seeded at the eclipse.

On 7 May, the first of three conjunctions (May, August and November) occurred between asteroid Juno and Uranus. This alignment occurs every five years, but was particularly significant coming a few days after the major conjunction above. Juno brings the principle of 'Right Relationship', first with ourselves, on all levels, and then with others. Juno plays a particularly important role in 2012. To be in Right Relationship, we need to release all negative attachments to the past, so we do not repeat patterns of relating that are rooted in reactions to our upbringing, past relationships or past lives. This includes releasing attitudes and behaviour that do not honour our self-worth. When we truly honour ourselves, we move naturally toward right relations with others.

In the midst of the Juno–Uranus alignments, there was a grand conjunction between Jupiter and Saturn in Taurus on

28 May. This occurs every 20 years, enabling new visions and ideals (Jupiter) to come into manifestation (Saturn). This had the effect of 'amplifying' everything being birthed by the 'stellium' of seven planets and the Juno–Uranus alignment.

Varuna – Keeper of Cosmic Order

On 28 November 2000, a small Kuiper Belt Object (KBO) was discovered, orbiting within the inner and outer limits of Pluto's highly elliptical orbit. It was given the name of an important Hindu deity, Varuna. As master of the rhythms of Cosmic Order (*Rta*) and the upholder of truth and spiritual law, Varuna governs the cycles of the Celestial Ocean (the night sky), and the sky, rain and oceans.

In the Hindu Vedas, Varuna is all-knowing. The stars are his many eyes, watching every aspect of human affairs; we can see the negative side of this in the 'Big Brother' surveillance society. Varuna's positive goal is to ensure that we uphold truth and integrity in all of our affairs, so that *our* actions on Earth reflect the Cosmic Order. Varuna's discovery 'raised the game' and brought the need for new levels of integrity in all of our dealings with each other. Varuna also brought awareness that we have it within our power to call others to account when they act dishonestly or without integrity – there have been many examples of this since.

Alignments 2001

A highly significant event of 2001 was the attack on the World Trade Center in New York on 11 September. This has redefined the world situation ever since, with ongoing ramifications. To explore it from an astrological perspective may bring an understanding of its inner significance.

Since July 2001, increasingly intense and polarized planetary patterns had been developing. On the 21 June Solstice there was a Total Solar Eclipse over southern Africa. It is rare for a Solar Eclipse to occur on a Solstice because of the precessional movement. This particular Solstice Eclipse occurred at the intersection of the Ecliptic and the Galactic Equator, exactly opposite to the December Solstice and Galactic Equator intersection point. This unusual alignment of Solar Eclipse, Solstice and Galactic Equator had a profound significance.

In the Star Map on page 86, see how the upstretched hand of Orion was 'holding' the Moon and Sun, symbolically bringing the impulse from the Galactic Equator through the 'doorway' of the eclipse into the constellation of Orion, and anchoring it into the Celestial Equator at Orion's Belt.

The pyramids of Egypt are the representation on Earth of the three stars of Orion's Belt[6]. In Egyptian mythology, Orion is identified with Osiris. Osiris and his brother Set represent the spiritual and earthly aspects of the same being. Osiris was murdered by his more earthly counterpart Set, who cut his body into pieces and scattered them throughout Egypt. This resulted in Osiris becoming the archetype of the wounded God-king; his wounding resulted from his 'descent' into the material world and the ensuing separation between the spiritual and instinctual/sexual aspects of his being. It fell to Isis, his sister-wife, to restore Osiris/Orion to wholeness. The feminine heart and womb of Isis held the key to healing the wound, and she eventually gave birth to the new God-king child, Horus.

This eclipse, by realigning our Earth, Moon and Sun with the Galactic Equator, and the mythology of Osiris/Orion,

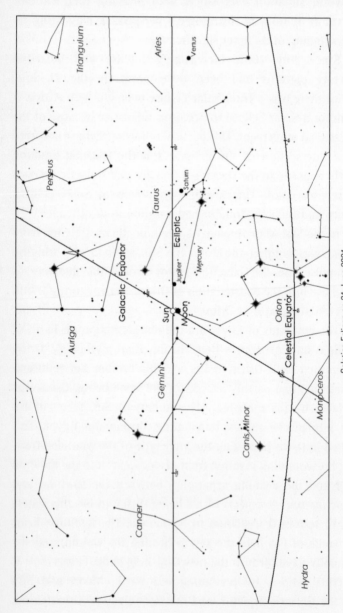

Solstice Eclipse on 21 June 2001

Image produced by Chris Marriott's SkyMap Pro

accelerated the process of healing the split between the spiritual and the instinctual expressions of the male Will. Inevitably, after a major healing impulse of this nature, there followed a global healing crisis, and period of purification; it often appears that things are getting much worse, as the 'symptoms' of an underlying imbalance are brought to the surface, like a homoeopathic reaction, on a global scale!

Osiris/Orion is an expression of the 'First Ray of Creation'[7] that manifests Divine Will into our human realm. The eclipse began the healing of our collective expression of the First Ray, which is the Ray of Spiritual Power. This energy is transmuted by the star *'Alkaid'*, in Ursa Major, (the Great Bear or Big Dipper). Each of the seven stars of Ursa Major is said to transmute the high spiritual frequencies of one of the 'Seven Rays of Creation', so that our human consciousness can assimilate them.

Alkaid is Arabic for 'governor' or 'leader', corresponding with the concept of pure will, emanating from a Divine Source, similar to the spiritual impulse received through the highest point of a pyramid. *Al Qaeda*, also Arabic, means the 'foundation', or 'base' of the pyramid. Both are expressions of the First Ray energy of Spiritual Power. The challenge with the First Ray is that once it begins its descent from pure spirit, down through the levels of manifestation, its creative power can become corrupted through an overly rigid or dogmatic interpretation of its Divine Will energy, which can result in violence or oppression.

Following the powerful June Solstice Eclipse, the events of 9/11 amplified our awareness of the need to confront the powerful and uncompromising energies of the First Ray, in both its negative and positive expressions. Its devastatingly negative expression on 9/11 set us on a course toward understanding the *right* use of such power – inevitably, this produced some very wrong expressions of that power, most notably in the reasons created for initiating the war in Iraq.

The astrology of 9/11 revealed a potential for positive transformation. Jupiter, near the Midheaven, brought hope, born out of confrontation with the deepest inner truths and wisdom of the soul. This was an opportunity for the world's most powerful and influential countries to awaken to a new archetype of the male spiritual warrior, and to find new, creative, more heart-centred ways for the resolution of conflicts. Clearly, there is still a way to go with this! At a personal level many people are beginning to approach this and apply it in their lives. At the political level, on the whole, we have witnessed the same old destructive expressions of the Mars energy. However, these are gradually being understood to be ineffective, inappropriate and counterproductive, feeding rather than resolving the world's power problems.

A Galactic Centre Alignment

Astronomers believe that at the heart of the Galactic Centre is a 'supermassive' black hole, known as Sagittarius A*. This lies on the Galactic Equator, below the Ecliptic, between the constellations of Sagittarius and Scorpio, and below the constellation of Ophiuchus.

Our perspective of the Galactic Centre moves 1° every 72 years, due to Precession. In 2001, it was at 26° 52' Sagittarius.

On 14 November 2001, asteroid Pallas Athene was conjunct with Chiron, both less than 1° away from the position of the Galactic Centre. This was the first of several planetary alignments with the GC, between 1999 and 2012. Pallas and Chiron were both in Ophiuchus as they became conjunct.

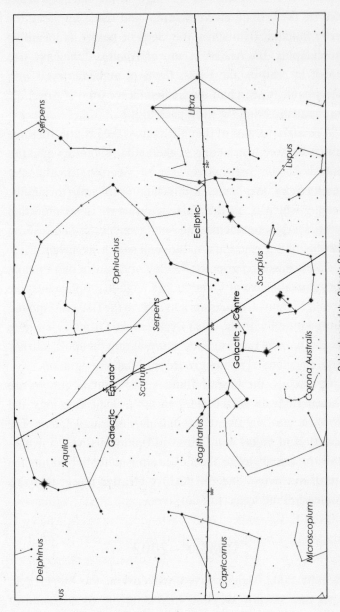

Ophiuchus and the Galactic Centre

Image produced by Chris Marriott's SkyMap Pro

Ophiuchus is the missing '13th sign' of the Sidereal Zodiac, straddling the Ecliptic above Scorpio, and rising up along the Galactic Equator. Ophiuchus, the 'Serpent Bearer' is identified as Aesculapius, the healer[8], a son of Apollo. Ophiuchus was educated by Chiron, the wisest Centaur, and journeyed with the Argonauts in search of the Golden Fleece (Age of Aries). He could reputedly bring the dead back to life.

Although the stars of Ophiuchus cross the Ecliptic, for some reason it became lost as one of the zodiac signs; its qualities remained in the redemptive side of Scorpio, traditionally represented by the eagle. Ophiuchus' stars link to Aquila, the eagle, which is on the Galactic Equator. This connection between Scorpio, Ophiuchus and Aquila enables us to transform the depths of our emotional nature and soar heavenwards.

Ophiuchus is represented holding and controlling Ophion, the primordial snake of Creation (see page 91). Ophiuchus, the self-realized human, stands upright next to the Galactic Equator, aligning himself with the Great Cycles of the Cosmos. He wields the snake, parallel to the Ecliptic, representing the soul's journey through the material planes toward spiritual reintegration.

Ophiuchus, the Cosmic Human, understands how to use the healing powers of the Spirit to bring body, emotions and mind back into alignment through pure spiritual intent. The conjunction of Pallas and Chiron in Ophiuchus, was a 'wake-up call' to acknowledge the full healing potential within the centre of our being, and the positive creative power that this can unleash in all aspects of our lives.

Quaoar – 2002

On 4 June 2002, Quaoar was discovered in the Kuiper Belt, with its tiny satellite Weywot, traversing the constellation of

Ophiuchus and Serpens

From Urania's Mirror constellation cards, published c.1825, reproduced courtesy of OldBookArt.com

Ophiuchus. In December 2012, Quaoar will be just 3° from the Galactic Centre.

Quaoar is a Native American creation deity of the Tongva people in California. In their mythology, Quaoar sang and danced the world into existence. As in other creation myths, first there was Chaos then Quaoar appeared. He was saddened by the emptiness of the Void, so he began to dance and sing the Song of Creation.

His dance created Weywot, God of the Sky (Ouranos) and Chehooit, Goddess of the Earth (Gaia). They joined in with the dance, to create the Sun and the Moon. Together, these five sang and danced everything else into existence. When the Creation was complete, Quaoar returned back to where he came from.

Quaoar's discovery in Ophiuchus brings a new level of healing to the deep wounds within the human psyche, which have kept us locked in the collective belief that we are separate from Creation. The 'teachings' of many religions that we are in some way to blame for that perceived separation, have given rise to deeply ingrained levels of conscious and unconscious guilt.

It is deeply significant that a Native American god was chosen for this planetoid. Native American spirituality is rooted in the knowledge that Earth is a Spiritual Being, in contrast to many religions that hold the dualistic belief of a split between our Heavenly and Earthly natures.

Quaoar's discovery offers hope, reminding us that the whole Universe is sacred and that we never actually separated from Oneness. The belief that we *were* separate, however, has prevented us from experiencing the Bliss of Oneness. Quaoar reminds us to dance our own Creation in every moment, so that our dance of life brings us Bliss.

Mars Approaches – 2003

On 27 August 2003, Mars came closer to the Earth than it had been for nearly 60,000 years, the time when Neanderthals walked on the Earth. It never appeared 'as large as the Moon', as many viral emails claimed; those same emails have re-circulated every August since! This reminds us of the need for discernment in these matters.

Mars was aligned with Uranus, bringing the energy of breakthrough to help release the old patterns of the Destructive Warrior and realign the archetypes of the Spiritual Warrior and the Wise Man. This was yet another stage in bringing the First Ray frequencies of Spiritual Will more fully into our human consciousness.

In coming close to us, Mars brought the positive, creative frequencies of a focused and more spiritually aligned use of the personal will. Aligning with Uranus, it challenged the methods applied universally toward conflict resolution. Together they represented the heroic journey of the Spiritual Warrior to overcome inner fears and embrace self-awareness.

Sedna Emerges from the Depths – 2003

On 14 November 2003, Sedna was discovered in the furthest reaches of the Solar System. Its highly elliptical orbit extends out to 32 times the distance of Neptune. To date, it is the most distant Dwarf Planet known to be orbiting our Sun.

Sedna is an Inuit sea goddess, queen of the Deep Ocean or Underworld. She was the mermaid-like daughter of the creator-god Anguta and became so huge and hungry that she ate everything, even gnawing off one of her father's arms while he slept. He was so enraged that he threw her over the side of his canoe but she clung on, so he chopped off her fingers until she let go. She sank down to become the Queen of the Deep and her enormous fingers became the seals, sea lions and whales.

In other myths Sedna was a beautiful maiden, lured into marriage by an evil bird spirit. When her father tried to rescue her, the spirit caused a terrible storm, threatening the survival of her people. In desperation, her father threw her into the sea.

The common theme in the Sedna myths is that she died at the hands of her father, either as an innocent victim or as a punishment. The stories agree that she descended into the depths of the ocean and became the Goddess of Sea Creatures. Thus the hunters and their families were dependent on the benevolence of Sedna for their survival.

Sedna represents the dark, devouring aspect of the Goddess, similar to the Hindu Kali. She rules the depths of the Collective Unconscious that, if ignored or rejected, can threaten to overwhelm us. To deal with this deep level of the Unconscious, we need first to have confronted its more accessible, shallower levels, signified by Saturn and Pluto. Once we begin to own our spiritual will (Pluto), we can learn how to align with the natural rhythms of Cosmic Order (*Rta*), signified by Varuna; and then reclaim our power as co-creators with Quaoar, our inner spiritual Source.

Once we know our true power as co-creators, then we can redeem the most hidden and potentially destructive elements of our Collective Shadow (Sedna). When we dare to embrace the Dark Feminine within us, there is an abundance of creativity to be released. When Sedna rises up into our consciousness, our initial reaction may be to run away or try to destroy her. But she requires us to confront the deepest aspects of the self-destructive denial of our spiritual nature, and acknowledge that we are wholly dependent upon the cycles of the Earth and the Cosmos for our survival.

Orcus Appears – 2004

On 17 February 2004, Orcus was discovered in the Kuiper Belt, its orbit a 'mirror image' of Pluto's.

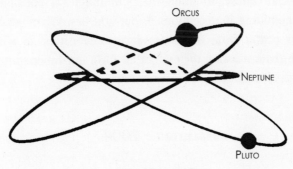

Orbits of Orcus and Pluto

In Roman Mythology, Pluto, Orcus and Dis Pater ('wealthy father') are three aspects of the same god of the Underworld. He is the Greek Phorcys, pre-dating Poseidon (Neptune) as primeval god of the sea and god of the Dead. His wife Keto gave birth to hideous monsters, including the Graeae and the Gorgons. To the Romans, Orcus represented the darkest qualities of the God of the Underworld, punishing evildoers, especially those guilty of breaking oaths.

Orcus is highly significant, as we struggle with the worldwide effects of broken oaths, following the near collapse of the banking system in 2008. This was followed by the breaking of manifesto 'oaths' by governments, when they realized the true depth of the economic mess we were in. Orcus is currently below Virgo in the constellation of Hydra, the 'many-headed monster'. He is revealing the 'many-headed monsters' of modern government bureaucracies, banks and multinational corporations. We learn from mythology that the Hydra cannot be killed by simply cutting off its heads because new ones just keep growing – like the bankers' bonuses! The Hydra can only be subdued by stabbing it directly in the heart.

Orcus challenges us to confront that aspect of the Collective Shadow that chooses to ignore the truth or deny responsibility, thereby colluding in deceptions or outright lies. When we take back our power from the 'many-headed monsters' to which we have given it away, then we bring forth our inner spiritual wealth (Dis Pater).

Haumea – 2004

In contrast to the dark Orcus, the bright Haumea was next to be discovered on 28 December 2004 at Mauna Kea observatory in Hawaii. Haumea is one of the strangest objects in the Solar System; shaped like a cigar, she spins end over end, giving the appearance of continually changing her shape.

Mythologically, Haumea is the Hawaiian Mother Goddess, who gave birth to the Cosmos from the primordial slime. She is the Mother to Pele, the creatrix and volcano goddess. Haumea is a 'shape-shifter', having the power to transform herself from youth to age and back again. So, she manifests Mother Earth's capacity for self-renewal, throughout history and particularly during the changing of the ages.

It appears that Haumea was in a huge collision in the distant past, as she has two moons and five smaller parts orbiting with her – there are eight pieces of Haumea and there are eight islands of Hawaii!

The discovery of Haumea began the process of preparing us to receive the universal healing energies of Chiron and Neptune, which would align directly over Hawaii in 2010, and significant planetary alignments occurring over Hawaii during the two Solar Eclipses in 2012 (see Chapters 5 and 6).

Eris, Bringer of Strife – 2005

Next to be discovered, on 5 January 2005, was Eris. It is the largest known Dwarf Planet, slightly larger than Pluto, and orbits in the 'Scattered Disc', beyond the Kuiper Belt. Eris is certainly a force to be reckoned with.

Eris' highly inclined orbit places it in the constellation of Cetus, south of the ecliptic constellations of Pisces and Aries. Cetus is the Sea Monster, which according to Bernadette Brady represents 'the unknown beast from the depths rather than what we know as the gentle giant of the sea'[9], the whale. Cetus brought devastation to ancient Aethiopia and was slain by Perseus when he rescued Andromeda from being devoured. Eris' discovery in this constellation fits with her mythological meaning as the bringer of Strife and Discord.

Eris, like Sedna, represents a rejected aspect of the Dark Goddess. She is rejected when we lose our understanding of the deeper laws of the Cosmos and the psyche, and when we forget how to honour the spiritual within the physical. This forgetting brings discord, created by distorted perceptions of the spiritual. At one extreme this may manifest as fanaticism or religious fundamentalism; at the other, as atheistic or scientific fundamentalism – all totally convinced that they and they alone are right, unwilling to tolerate other viewpoints.

We can also see Eris at work in human affairs as terrorism, imperialism and as the chaos resulting from the greed and arrogance that brought about the banking crisis – a kind of 'financial terrorism', with little regard for the indiscriminate effects that the greed of the few would have upon the livelihoods of the many.

Eris brings to light hidden discords from deep within the Collective Psyche that have arisen from having focused on the purely material and caused us to lose our true inner values. This has created a 'monster' that is affecting the whole planet, ecologically, financially and spiritually. Eris is there to wake us up and lead us to rediscover something more fundamental and permanent within our nature.

Hesiod describes two aspects to Eris in *Works and Days*[10], as one 'fosters evil war and the fray of battle', while the other 'is much better, and she stirs even the shiftless to work... This Strife is good for mortals'. In other words, Eris can prompt us toward positive action to find the hidden possibilities within discord and make the world a better place. Athena had some very useful advice about the destructive Strife of Eris: 'If you just leave it alone, it stays small; but if you decide to fight it, then it swells from its small size and grows large.'

Makemake (*Ma'kay'ma'kay*) – 2005

Makemake, the third largest Dwarf Planet (after Eris and Pluto) was discovered on 31 March 2005. Makemake's discovery at Easter resulted in it being named after the creator god of Rapa Nui (Easter Island) in the South Pacific.

Makemake was the creator of humanity, a fertility god, and is depicted as a man with a bird's head and tail on hundreds of petroglyphs across Easter Island.

Makemake's orbit is highly inclined to the Ecliptic; it was in the constellation of Coma Berenices when it was discovered. Coma Berenices (Berenice's Hair) is the constellation that lies at the Galactic North Pole; in other words, Makemake was at the Galactic Crown Chakra when it was discovered.

This is the first of these new discoveries to be named after a mythology from Earth's southern hemisphere. This links us back to the ancient Polynesian cultures that spread throughout the Pacific, whose origins are said to extend far back to ancient Lemuria.

The naming of Makemake and its discovery at the Galactic Crown Centre brings the possibility for a collective 'remembering' of the deepest origins of humanity and of ways to live that were in perfect harmony with the natural world. These ancient ways were kept for millennia, until the arrival of Europeans in the Pacific. Fortunately, their memory is still preserved intact within the Kahuna traditions of Hawaii, and other present-day Pacific cultures. If we approach these with humility and respect, then we may learn to remember how to live in this way.

Chapter 5
THE STAGE IS SET (2006–10)

So the stage was set, with a whole new pantheon of Creator gods out in the far reaches of the Solar System. The characters were assembling, ready for the final act in the unfolding drama of 2012, although it may be that other 'players' have yet to appear.

Before the discovery of the 'new' planetoids and Dwarf Planets, their qualities were once all considered to be associated with the small but powerful Pluto. Pluto's discovery in 1930 had begun to make us aware of the inner processes of psychological transformation, regeneration and spiritual rebirth. Outwardly, it brought us into the atomic age, heralding a new world order based on our potential to unleash unspeakable power.

Pluto brings the choice of how we use power; we can use power to control, dominate and destroy or we can choose to awaken our inner potential to manifest the full creative power of our Spirit. This requires us to pass through the catharsis of confrontation with our personal Shadow (Saturn); then to confront the awesome power of the Collective Shadow (Pluto), which manifests in areas where we have given away, or allowed our personal power to be taken from us.

The most obvious manifestation of Pluto's negative power was the nuclear arms race and the subsequent threat of mutual annihilation between gargantuan but clearly defined 'opponents'. In 1989, the triple conjunction of Saturn and Neptune triggered the collapse of the Soviet Union and the breaching of the Berlin Wall. We witnessed the mass of the people (Neptune) quite literally flowing over the barrier (Saturn) that had been erected in 1961. This changed the power structure of the world. Neptune was responsible for the dissipation and confusion that followed; the once clearly focused and easily identified threat had dissipated. At least we had known before who 'the enemy' was. 'We' were right and 'they' were wrong – it was all very clear... to both sides!

The 'new' Planetoids and Dwarf Planets beyond Pluto are defining and differentiating the subtle, mysterious, and often challenging qualities 'lurking' within the depths of the collective psyche. Since Roman times, the major planets have been known to the Western world by the names of Roman deities. Now, we are encountering a group of new (to us), but very ancient Creator gods from diverse cultures, ranging from the Inuit of the Arctic Circle (Sedna), to the inhabitants of the South Pacific (Makemake).

The traditional planets out to Saturn concern our individual processes and destinies in this world; those from Chiron out to Pluto concern our spiritual awakening, while the 'new' gods represent collective qualities within global consciousness. Pluto lies at the threshold between the individual and the collective, between the previously known Solar System and the far reaches of consciousness in its outskirts.

Many of the darker collective qualities, once attributed to Pluto, are now held by beings such as Orcus and Eris, leaving Pluto free to rediscover his divine origins. Pluto was an Olympian god, who *chose* to take responsibility for the Underworld. Now it is time for him to bring his divine connection back into collective awareness, in preparation for 2012. This process began when Pluto aligned with the Galactic Centre three times in 2006 and 2007. But first there was some clearing of the past to do.

2006 Eclipsing the Roots of Western Civilization

On 29 March 2006, a Total Solar Eclipse began over Recife, the most easterly point of Brazil. It swept across the Atlantic, making landfall over West Africa. Maximum eclipse occurred over Libya then crossed Turkey and Kazakhstan, to finish north of Mongolia (see page 104).

As with the 1999 Eclipse, there is too much information to explore fully here. A crucial detail was that the shadow passed exactly over Çatalhöyük in Turkey, on the same day as Pluto turned retrograde. This eclipse marked the final stage in the process of releasing any negative energetic threads that had become inexorably 'woven' into the fabric of human consciousness, since the establishment of the first modern city-state at Çatalhöyük around 9,500 years ago.

Pluto turned retrograde, just before aligning with the Galactic Centre in December 2006, making one last foray into the unconscious depths, to release the more destructive tendencies of our personal and collective will. It was as if Pluto symbolically took a step back to get a good run up toward the Galactic Centre! Just as many layers of successive civilizations, each built on top of another, have been unearthed at Çatalhöyük, so this eclipse was an opportunity to unearth the psychological

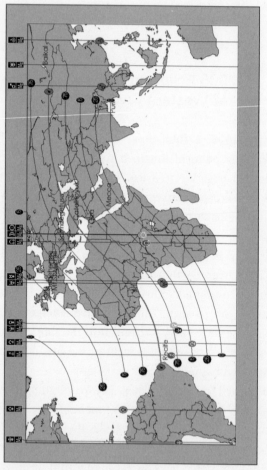

Path of March 2006 Eclipse over Çatalhöyük

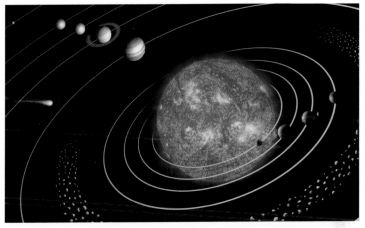

Plate 1 – The Planets and the Ecliptic Plane
Image by NASA/JPL

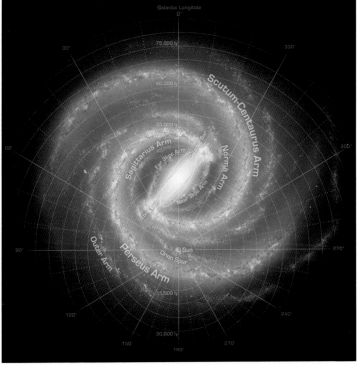

Plate 2 – Milky Way Galaxy
Image by NASA

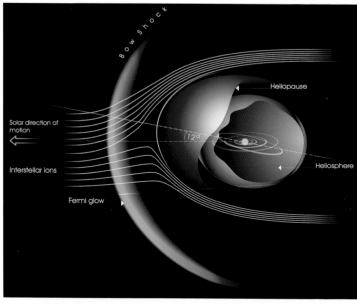

Plate 3 – The Heliosphere

Image by ESA & Lotfi Ben Jaffel (Institut d'Astrophysique de Paris (CNRS-INSU)), Martin Kornmesser and Lars Lindberg Christensen (Space Telescope-European Coordination Facility)

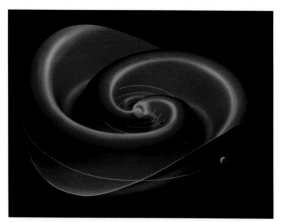

Plate 4 – Heliospheric Current Sheet – 'Ballerina Skirt'

Image by NASA artist Werner Heil

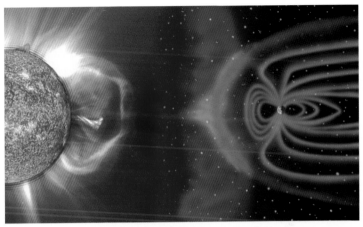

Plate 5 – The Solar Wind & Earth's Magnetic Field
Image by NASA

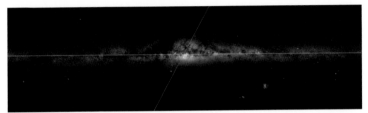

Plate 6 – Panoramic Milky Way Galaxy with Galactic Equator (white) and Ecliptic plane (red)
ESO/S. Brunier

Plate 7 – Kukulkan Pyramid, Chichen Itza, Mexico
Photo: Marcus Mason © 2009

Plate 8 – 'Summer Milky Way', showing the constellation of Sagittarius and the
Galactic 'Dark Rift', the *Xibalba-be*, Road to the Underworld

Photo: Anthony Ayiomamitis, © 2001–2011, reproduced with permission

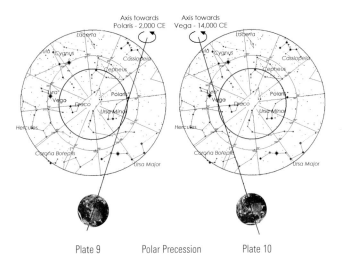

Plate 9   Polar Precession   Plate 10
Currently – towards Polaris   14,000 CE – towards Vega

Star maps produced by Chris Marriott's SkyMap Pro; Earth image – NASA; image compiled by M. Mason

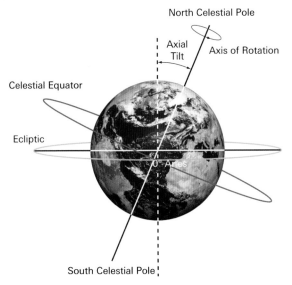

Plate 11 – Ecliptic & Celestial Equator intersect at 0° Aries

Adapted from picture by Dennis Nilsson; Earth image – istockphoto.com

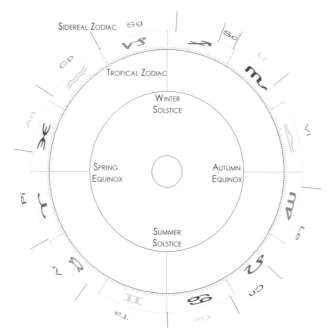

Plate 12 – Tropical and Sidereal Zodiacs

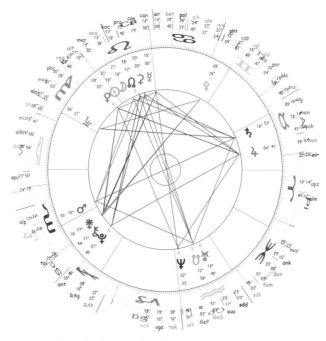

Plate 13 – Geocentric Total Solar Eclipse 11 August 1999

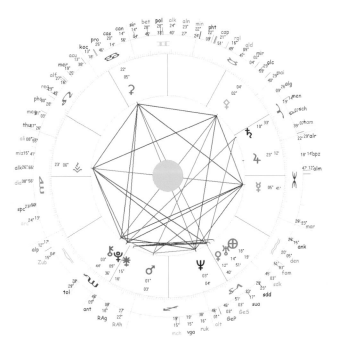

Plate 14 – Heliocentric Total Solar Eclipse 11 August 1999

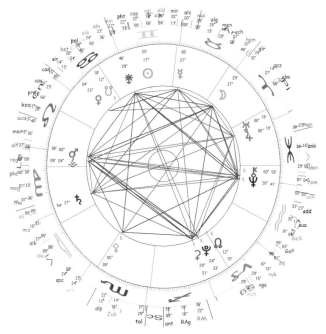

Plate 15 – Jupiter–Uranus Conjunction 8 June 2010

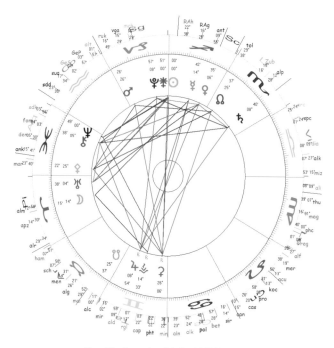

Plate 16 – December Solstice 2012 Geocentric

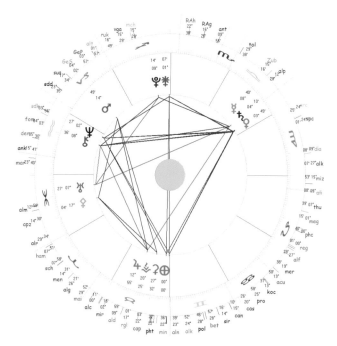

Plate 17 – December Solstice 2012 Heliocentric

layers that have created our modern culture. It is important to acknowledge the good and the positive, but also to own up to negative and destructive behaviour patterns that were generated, particularly in our attitude toward our environment, once we became 'civilized'.

Pluto Aligns with the Galactic Centre – 2006–07

At its core, Pluto's purpose is to bring us awareness and acceptance of the power of our inner spiritual Light, our spiritual Will. Pluto challenges our ego to align will with our spiritual will, the inner drive to fulfil our destiny. In doing this, Pluto also reveals how we may align with Universal, or Divine Will.

In other words, Pluto's role is to help us move beyond our ego desires and discover what we need to do and be, in order to fulfil our deepest yearning for a sense of purpose. It is not necessary to have any particular spiritual or religious belief; it is more a question of finding what it is in our life that just feels 'right' and true from the very core of our being. First we need to be able to experience our core, the inner, fundamental, atomic substance of our 'I am' consciousness. This is not the ego consciousness of 'I am this' or 'I am that'; it is not dependent on the roles we play in the world. It is simply the consciousness that 'I am', 'I exist', 'I am self-aware'.

This awareness connects us to the core of our being. Once we confront our fears and strip our ego of all that is not an expression of our core, then we may experience the pure, clear, powerful light of just Being. Pluto is only a disruptive force in our lives when we are in denial of our Light. With a very few enlightened exceptions, most people are in denial of this, at some level. So, it is no surprise that Pluto is a force to be reckoned with; it can appear to be destructive, but Pluto only ever destroys aspects of our false ego.

Pluto aligned with the Galactic Centre three times, in December 2006, and in July and October 2007. The Galactic Centre is the motivating force behind the movement and revolution of the galaxy through space. It lies at the heart of the largest single organism that we inhabit. If we can learn to align and adapt our consciousness to the rhythms and cycles of the Solar System *and* the galaxy, then we will truly become 'Galactic Beings'. This is what is becoming possible, as we approach December 2012.

As Pluto aligned with the Galactic Centre it challenged everyone on the planet to rediscover their innermost purpose, and to align that with the purpose of the larger Whole. We can express this using many different terms, depending on our beliefs – aligning with 'Divine Will', or a 'Higher Power', or 'Universal Will', 'Cosmic Will', 'God', 'Great Spirit', 'Christ-consciousness', and so on.

Pluto's alignment with the Galactic Centre effectively 'plugged us into the mainframe' and began the process of bringing all aspects of our being back into alignment. It set the conditions to create an unbroken thread from the pure Light of our Being, through our mental and emotional levels, through the physical body and into the Earth.

The Galactic Centre, Pluto and Earth were lined up, all resonating to the same frequency, re-establishing the connection between the Galactic Centre and the Earth's Core[1]. Humans are the intermediaries for that process. The more we become conscious of the link between the Core of the Galaxy and the Core of the Earth, the more we will understand how to honour the Earth as our true Physical Mother and the galaxy as our Cosmic Mother; they are aspects of the same Being.

Juno Aligns with the Galactic Centre – 2008

In 2008, Juno aligned with the Galactic Centre in March, May and October. Juno teaches the principle of 'Right Relations'. Her alignments 'tested' our ability to express our newly acquired connection between the GC and Mother Earth.

This was also the year when many 'wrong relations' came to light. Most notable was our global relationship with debt and greed. We experienced how the banking system had created a dysfunctional global family; the following year in the UK, the widespread abuse of MP's Parliamentary expenses revealed the institutionalized abuse of a relationship of trust.

Juno was 'calling in' the highest demands for spiritual integrity, which need to become the norm, if we are to successfully negotiate the current changes, and truly become co-creators of a fairer, more loving and compassionate world.

When planets align with the GC, they connect their highest possible expression into the core of our being, so that any dishonesty or corruption 'lurking' in our unconscious motivations will come to light. At a personal level, it is becoming increasingly uncomfortable for us to live without expressing high levels of personal integrity and honesty. At national, governmental and global levels, organizations and regimes that do not embody high levels of integrity, honesty and the true interests of their citizens are inevitably failing. If these organizations and their leaders do not understand the concept of 'Right Relations', then their political lives will be very short lived.

It is significant that Pluto and Juno were both above the Ecliptic in the constellation of Ophiuchus when they aligned with the Galactic Centre. They were awakening our highest aspirations to live from a place of spiritual integrity, to release and heal any attachments to negative emotional patterns, based on fear or control. While Juno set the conditions for these new levels of integrity, other alignments were to come along to ensure that we got the point!

Jupiter Aligns with Chiron and Neptune – 2009

Chiron had been creating an enticing cosmic dance with Neptune since the beginning of 2008, as they moved closer, then went retrograde and moved apart, then came closer again. This was preparing us for a profound level of healing, when they became exactly conjunct in February 2010; in the meantime, Jupiter came along to align with them both during 2009.

Jupiter brings the awareness of new possibilities, opens us to a new vision for the future and brings feelings of hope and optimism. As Jupiter aligned with Chiron and Neptune in May, July and December, it began to awaken in our hearts the vision of how we would like to live. In its retrograde phase (June–August), it also showed us what was still preventing the realization of our vision. The challenge was to surrender our ideas of what *we* wanted, release all ego-generated illusions, and allow the Universe to show us the way forward through the healing power of unconditional love.

The combined energies of Jupiter and Neptune are vast. Jupiter is physically the largest planet in the Solar System, with its magnetic field completely dwarfing the size of the Sun itself (see diagram on page 109).

Neptune connects us with the infinity of space and the formlessness of the spiritual worlds. With these two planets acting together, their endless possibilities could leave us overwhelmed or confused.

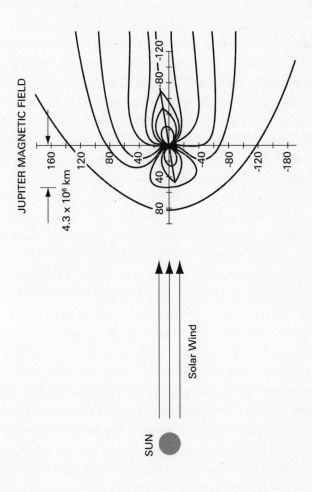

Jupiter's Magnetic Field
Adapted from a NASA image

Surrendering our limited ideas and perceptions about our life and its possibilities, while allowing inner guidance to flow from the core of our being, can enable a true vision for our future to emerge. Jupiter is motivated by what is for the good of the Whole, as well as the individual. A vision that emerges from the depths of the Unconscious will show that what is right for us as individuals is also right for the larger whole; it will be in harmony with natural cycles. Everything in Nature has its role and place within the evolutionary purpose of the Whole, playing its part in sustaining the overall balance.

Humans are the only species on Earth with the free will to choose to go against Natural Law. We are experiencing the consequences of this through our contribution toward climate change. We have managed, in a few hundred years, to upset the natural balance of a planet that evolved by following naturally changing climate cycles over millions of years.

The alignments of Jupiter, Chiron and Neptune greatly increased global awareness of just how deeply we are wounding our planet. While Neptune may, at times, have made the whole 'problem' seem overwhelming, Jupiter's role is to offer us a vision of hope. This is not simply the hope for some magic scientific 'fix'; the true problem lies much deeper. Jupiter is bringing the awareness that what needs to change is our inner attitude toward our relationship with the Earth.

Since the dawn of 'civilization', and the arrival of the first city-states like Çatalhöyük in Asia Minor, during the Age of Cancer, we have been slowly and imperceptibly losing our intimate connection with the Spirit of the Earth. Before that, as hunter-gatherers, we had little choice but to follow the seasonal cycles and migrations. Humans knew that they were wholly dependent on Nature for all their needs. Despite the many advantages that come with 'civilization', city dwelling and the development of complex technologies, what has been lost is something far more precious. With the exception of a few undiscovered tribes in the rainforests, we have lost an appreciation of the real value of living in harmony with Nature.

Jupiter brought the promise that it is not too late to retrieve that connection. It brought the growing awareness that this process has to begin with ourselves. It is not enough to recycle our rubbish, to turn off lights and reduce our carbon emissions. That is a start, but there is an urgent need to remember how to *feel* our connection with the Earth and to feel the sheer wonder of being alive on this beautiful planetary being, floating through this exquisitely beautiful Cosmos.

Throughout 2009, Jupiter awakened the vision of living our sacred connection with the Earth and the Cosmos. Chiron was soon to reveal the healing possibilities that such awareness brings, as it approached conjunction with Neptune in February 2010.

Chiron and Neptune Align Over Hawaii – 2010

On 16 February 2010, Chiron and Neptune finally became conjunct, with their North–South Meridians aligned over Hawaii.

Their conjunction last occurred in 1945, two days after the end of World War II, also over the Pacific Ocean. Then, it heralded the promise of a new era of international relations and the slow beginnings of a global awakening to new levels of consciousness.

As they aligned in February 2010, Chiron and Neptune initiated a global awakening to the healing energies of

Unconditional Love. This alignment was essential to prepare us for the rebirth of spiritual consciousness in December 2012. Chiron and Neptune remain closely aligned until February 2013, when Chiron will slowly move 'out of orb' with Neptune. The doorway for us to receive and express increasingly profound levels of Unconditional Love will remain open until then. After that they will not be conjunct again until 2094.

Their February 2010 alignment heralded a global shift toward heart-centred awareness. In order to feel this, any structures that we had created in our lives, work and relationships, which were not a true expression of our heart, simply began to dissolve around us. This is the way of Neptune; it dissolves and removes limiting structures that no longer reflect our inner self, or keep us trapped in the Illusion that we are separate from others or from the Universe.

It also meant that structures within governments, banking and big business would be unsustainable unless they learned to become more compassionate. At the time of writing, we are experiencing the uncertainties of a world recession, with radical, even desperate, restructuring by governments, often with little regard for compassion. There is still a long way to go before these institutions understand how to work with the healing potentials of Chiron and Neptune.

Neptune can create situations where good intentions fail due to woolly thinking or lack of substance. But Chiron is uncompromising; when something needs to be healed, it will not rest until that is achieved. In this global healing crisis, all the ugliness, greed, double-dealing, deception, pretence and collusion that have been practised since the global restructuring of 1945, is coming to the surface. Now it is time for real change; the true power behind Neptune will ensure that happens relentlessly, yet compassionately. All that is required for the compassion to flow is a letting-go and a change of heart. If we act from a place of Right Action, with an intent that it is truly for the good of the whole, then we will freely and effortlessly receive the abundance of the Universe in every moment.

The Chiron–Neptune alignment over Hawaii had profound significance, as many regard Hawaii as one of the Earth's most important energy centres. It has been described as the planetary 'Alta Major' Centre[2]; in the human energy system, the Alta Major is the energy centre, or chakra at the bridge of the nose, and is rooted in the hypothalamus. This centre connects us to our deep ancestral and shamanic memory of our intimate connection with the energies and cycles of the natural world. Hawaii 'holds' this energy for the entire planet, so that whatever spiritual impulses 'imprint' there, they can flow to all parts of the globe; it is like a planetary Master Acupuncture point.

This unfolding process of change was greatly accelerated by three conjunctions between Jupiter and Uranus during 2010–11.

Jupiter Aligns with Uranus

These two magnificent planets become conjunct every 13 to 14 years. Always heralding new discoveries and scientific breakthroughs, they awaken us to new levels of awareness, can bring radical political change, and provide many personal 'Aha moments' and creative insights.

Jupiter and Uranus require that we see the big picture, so we can formulate plans that align with our deepest inner needs. As always with Uranus, this means letting go of whatever no longer works in our lives. Even when this seems impossible, it is necessary to remain receptive toward unexpected opportunities that can enable quantum leaps of consciousness.

The Jupiter–Uranus conjunction made us more aware of the possibilities for positive change and healing that were heralded by Chiron and Neptune. Some quantum physicists are telling us that matter does not exist, only consciousness. This implies that our collective consciousness can influence the behaviour of matter. If enough people choose to express clarity, wisdom and compassion, then we will live in a clear, wise and loving world – it seems so simple!

On 8 June 2010, Jupiter and Uranus were conjunct in the first degree of Aries, signifying new beginnings at personal and planetary levels. The last time their alignment occurred in Aries was in 1927–28; Richard Tarnas, in his inspiring *Cosmos and Psyche*, describes this as 'the conjunction that occurred at the climax of the quantum physics revolution that was marked by Bohr's principle of complementarity, Heisenberg's principle of indeterminacy, and the Solvay congress of October 1927'[3]. This was the first conference where the world's leading physicists, such as Einstein and Bohr, discussed quantum theory. Tarnas also points out that this was the same year that the first 'talkie', *The Jazz Singer*, appeared, the first television transmission was made between London and Glasgow and it was the year of Charles Lindberg's first solo trans-Atlantic flight.

In 2010, we saw a major shift toward 3D cinema, with the groundbreaking film *Avatar*. It seems likely that we can also expect astounding leaps in technology and particle physics, now that the Large Hadron Collider is up and running. Richard Tarnas also describes how the Jupiter–Uranus conjunctions in 1775–76 and 1788–89 acted as catalysts for the American and French Revolutions[4]. As the current Jupiter–Uranus alignment reached its culmination in early 2011, we were to see it initiating radical political changes in North Africa and the Middle East (see Chapter 6).

Some strikingly familiar patterns were apparent in the astrology chart for the first Jupiter–Uranus alignment in June 2010. This was to be the last big planetary conjunction in the approach toward 2012; this was the catalytic energy behind the final 'push' for the change, whose seeds were planted during the 1999 Eclipse. The patterns of the Jupiter–Uranus chart mirrored the patterns of the 1999 Eclipse – a Grand Cross and a Six-pointed Star. Now both patterns were present within the same Geocentric Chart (see Colour Plate 15). The potentials that were seeded at the 1999 Eclipse were finally able to fully come to Earth. The spiritual Star of Grace was integrating with the physical structures of the Grand Cross – or almost; there was still some unfinished business to attend to as the alignment worked its way through the remaining conjunctions in September 2010 and January 2011.

The Moon completed the six-pointed star, on the day of the first Jupiter–Uranus conjunction in June, creating a perfect resonance in our emotional bodies. This provided the blueprint for how to live from a place of balance between our inner heart (Vesta), our will (Mars), our intuitive knowing (Pallas Athene), an empowered relationship with the Earth (Pluto and Ceres), the understanding of what is needed to bring us back to wholeness (Neptune and Chiron) and maintain Right Relationship with 'all our relations' (Juno in Cancer). This perfect pattern lasted for just one day, giving a glimpse of what was becoming possible. It was like a snapshot that occurred 'in the twinkling of an eye', which is all it takes for Uranus to bring about deep change.

Jupiter–Uranus in the Grand Cross was the 'trigger' to awaken and motivate us to make these potentials a reality. As both planets went retrograde between August and November 2010, we had to dig deep to release old attachments, but with the promise that we could emerge into new levels of integration and wholeness after their final conjunction on 4 January 2011.

CHAPTER 6
THE FINAL APPROACH (2011–12)

The final Jupiter–Uranus alignment on 4 January 2011 was the trigger for a sequence of revolutionary changes, reminiscent of the political upheaval in Europe brought by the Saturn–Neptune alignments of 1989. During this time, we experienced the complete restructuring of the politics of Eastern Europe. In 2011 we saw profound changes occurring in North Africa and the Middle East.

Almost nine months after the Grand Cross and Six-pointed Star of the Jupiter–Uranus conjunction in June 2010, the February New Moon brought Jupiter and Uranus' energy for change into sharp focus, with a 'stellium' of Sun, Moon, Mercury, Ceres, Mars, Neptune and Chiron in Aquarius. This was like an echo of the Grand Conjunction of seven planets, which occurred nine months after the Grand Cross and Six-pointed Star of the 1999 Eclipse.

At that time, the seeds of new paradigms and archetypes had been planted and they began to emerge into consciousness in May 2000. In 2011, the seeds of a new vision of the way forward, planted at the Jupiter–Uranus alignment in June 2010, were emerging with full force, bringing dramatic and radical changes. On the world stage, this manifested quickly with the political changes, which began in Tunisia and Egypt.

With Uranus being radical and confrontational, these changes were not as smooth or without violence as the collapse of the Eastern Bloc had been. In true Uranian style, however, it was initially swift and uncompromising, and the message was clear: dishonesty, corruption and lack of integrity would not be tolerated, not matter what the cost. The people had spoken and stood up for themselves – a sobering lesson to politicians across the world.

The Jupiter–Uranus alignments throughout 2010 brought many challenges and surprises, awakening us to a clear and realistic vision for our future. To succeed, this vision had to be based on individual integrity, a deep sense of inner purpose and the hope for a more spiritually focused future. In formulating our vision, we were challenged to let go of old beliefs and expectations no longer based in the present. This was a painful process; it is relatively easy to let go of things, ideals or relationships, when we see they have outlived their purpose. It was not so easy, if we were still attached to those ideals, beliefs or relationships that may have once served us but were now becoming untenable. The key was to understand that whatever was happening was for the highest good of all. Although it may not always have been apparent, our appreciation of this would emerge during 2011.

The challenge was to release the Old and step into the New, without preconceptions, fixed ideas or expectations. Our willingness to do this would define how easy or difficult the overall transition would be for us individually. In Tunisia, Egypt and Libya, there were three very different examples of the consequences of leaders either knowing when to give way to the changing tide, or creating chaos and destruction by defiantly clinging to power. The negative, shadow expression of this inevitably became focused in Libya, which had been the focus for the 2006 maximum Eclipse. Effectively, the Libyan people took on responsibility for dealing with the unresolved shadow energies for the whole Middle East.

Throughout February all the planets, except Saturn and Juno, were focused within just over one quarter (94°) of the zodiac, from Venus at the end of Sagittarius to Jupiter, leading the way forward just inside Aries.

The protests in Tunisia, Egypt, Bahrain, Yemen and Libya were graphic expressions of the need to change old paradigms

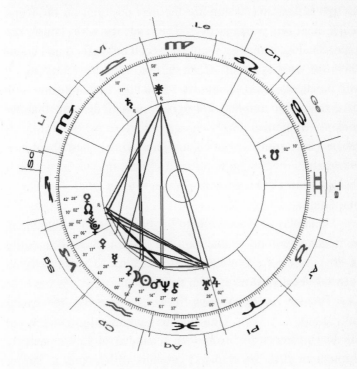

New Moon (Tunisia) on 3 February 2011 at 02:30 UT

of long-perpetuated patterns of 'wrong' relationship (Juno) and the structures and institutions (Saturn) that had been supporting these. Juno, the bringer of Right Relationship, was directly above Tunisia at the moment of New Moon.

The New Moon brought a unique moment in history, when President Mubarak of Egypt bowed to public pressure and resigned on 11 February 2011. John Simpson of BBC News remarked that this was the first time in 8,000 years that the Egyptian people had expressed what *they* wanted instead of taking orders from above.

Retrograde Juno and Saturn represent the 'unfinished business' that needs to be dealt with efficiently and effectively, so that it does not destabilize the new position, on the world stage or in our personal lives. The tendency with Saturn, our inner Shadow, is that we simply project it onto others and blame them for what is wrong. If we do this when it's retrograde, it will inevitably backfire, and we will simply exchange one form of tyranny for another. Retrograde planets demand that we look at our hidden, unconscious motivations; with Saturn, this means confronting fear of change, and being honest about how we frustrate or sabotage our own efforts, due to unconscious fears, narrow thinking or unwillingness to let go of what is safe and familiar.

Juno plays a crucial role in the December 2012 alignment, so it was important to maintain the highest levels of integrity in 2011, to ensure genuine Right Relations, to avoid carrying forward negative threads from the past.

The key to negotiating these changes was to remain fully awake in each moment, responding appropriately to all developments. We would be reminded of this repeatedly throughout 2011. The Sun was conjunct with Uranus at Spring Equinox, square (90°) Uranus at Summer Solstice, in opposition

(180°) to Uranus at Autumn Equinox, and square Uranus again at Winter Solstice. Each seasonal turning point was testing and challenging us to remain present and alert to the inner call for change, and to create firm foundations to support us as we approached 2012.

Uranus Square Pluto – 2011–15

2010 had been about incubating our vision; 2011 was about putting structures in place to enable us to live that vision. This became intensified by a square (90°) aspect between Uranus and Pluto that began during May 2011 and will last until May 2015. We were alerted to their approaching alignment by the nuclear disaster in Japan. At the physical level, this alignment creates a powerful tension between the right use of technology and power – in this instance, directly concerning the technology of Uranium and Plutonium, which triggered a worldwide debate about the wisdom of using nuclear power.

At the mental and spiritual levels, this alignment challenges us not only to apply our technological ingenuity toward solving the problems of how to generate enough physical power for our needs, but also how to apply real wisdom to the creation of power-structures in all aspects of life. Uranus in Aries wants to forge ahead with new ideas, new technologies, new systems of government and new approaches to spiritual awareness and understanding our place in the Cosmos. Pluto in Capricorn is more cautious, restrained, methodical, taking the long-term view, as it knows that whatever is changed now must be capable of enduring and supporting us into the future. The drawback with Pluto in Capricorn is that it can become too attached to the old structures and the power that gives to those who try to perpetuate those structures, even when it is clear that everything is breaking down.

The period 2011–15 will see much tension between these two powerful forces, as we try to create a balance between our eagerness for change and the need to apply our wisdom and experience in order to create long-term solutions for creating new and sustainable ways of being.

Grand Crosses in August

This dilemma became keenly focused as the Uranus–Pluto square was transformed into a Grand Cross by Mars and Juno between 2 and 15 August.

This intense combination challenged everyone to act with emotional integrity (Mars in Cancer), to let go of any tendency to dominate, control or manipulate others (Pluto in Capricorn), and to maintain Right Relations (Juno in Libra) by putting the needs of the group above individual needs (Uranus in Aries). This meant dealing with unfinished business with integrity and clarity, before we could move forward into the next phase of manifesting our vision.

This Grand Cross was further intensified when, on 5–6 August, the Moon (in Scorpio) formed another Grand Cross, with Vesta (in Aquarius), Jupiter (in Taurus) and Sun conjunct Venus (in Leo) (see page 123). This challenged us to confront the deepest wounds of the heart, in order to enable us to manifest truly balanced, creative relationships. The key was to feel the grief of our past, and move through that to reach a place of calm, serene, open-hearted acceptance.

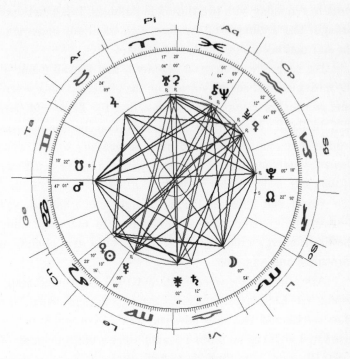

Two Grand Crosses in August 2011

2012 at Last!

In 2012, two powerful Solar Eclipses occur over the Pacific Ocean, which will allow the release of layers of energetic 'trauma imprints'.

The indigenous cultures of the Pacific have maintained an unbroken thread of memory of our Oneness with Mother Earth. This ancient wisdom is still carried within the Kahuna traditions of Hawaii. In February 2010, while on a sacred journey to Hawaii to work with the planetary healing potentials of the Chiron–Neptune alignment in February 2010, we were privileged to work in ceremony with two Hawaiian Kahunas. This experience brought just a glimpse of the deep, rich traditions underlying the spiritual history of the Pacific cultures.

We have already seen in Chapter 5 that Hawaii is one of the most powerful energy vortices on the planet – a place where new spiritual archetypes can anchor into the Earth and flow into the Earth's energy grids. It is crucial that the grid patterns around it remain as clear and pure as possible, so that what flows through here does not become distorted by the negativity of the past.

World War II in the Pacific brought much damage and destruction; extreme trauma was caused to the people and the Earth energy grids, by the dropping of atomic bombs on Hiroshima and Nagasaki.

After the war, between 1946 and 1958, the United States conducted 67 nuclear tests in the atmosphere above the Marshall Islands. The most powerful was a 15-megaton device detonated at Bikini Atoll on 1 March 1954 – the equivalent of 1,000 Hiroshimas. In total, these tests were equivalent to more than 7,000 Hiroshimas.

In 1969, the United States detonated a one-megaton nuclear weapon at Amchitka Island, in the Aleutian Islands that stretch west from Alaska toward Russia. A small group of protesters who tried to prevent this were to become the founders of Greenpeace[1].

In 2005 I travelled with a small group of friends to the volcanic Aleutian island of Akutan. The purpose of this journey was to work for planetary healing, focusing on the energetic effects of all the nuclear activity in the region. As we flew from Anchorage over the Aleutians I was overwhelmed by vast feelings of grief; other members of the group also experienced this in profound ways. What became clear was that many of the distortions in the Earth's energy grids, caused by the nuclear explosions, were then held in place by the imprints of painful human emotions. These distortions in Earth's subtle energy prevent us from fully receiving the new Light frequencies flowing into the Earth. Solar Eclipses offer opportunities to release these stuck emotions, to aid the healing processes of the Earth grids and thereby heal ourselves, too.

The two eclipses in 2012 bring the potential to release much more than the after-effects of World War II. They release negative patterns, created by centuries of abuse of the indigenous peoples of the Pacific. The eclipses are also releasing and healing damage caused to these spiritual traditions by the arrival of European explorers and missionaries, who imposed their dualistic notions of a split between Spirit and Matter.

The eclipses are significant for everyone on the planet, as they offer opportunities to release our collective planetary grief over the loss of our deep spiritual knowing of Oneness with Mother Earth and all of Creation.

Solar Annular Eclipse (20 May 2012)

Annular eclipses occur when the Moon is positioned further from the Earth and does not completely obscure the Sun, but leaves a ring (annulus) of light around the Moon's dark disk. It means that the Eclipse Shadow does not touch the surface of the Earth, but remains up in the atmosphere. Its effect is more on the subtle energy bodies of the Earth, at the mental and spiritual levels.

This eclipse begins 270 miles west of Hong Kong, and passes over Hong Kong, north of Taiwan and over Tokyo. It then arcs up near the Aleutian Islands for Maximum Eclipse, makes landfall north of San Francisco, crosses into Nevada, Utah and New Mexico, ending on the Texas border.

The eclipse 'triggers' a mental–spiritual release over the main financial centres of the Far East, before passing over the northernmost edge of the San Andreas Fault in California and then the 'Four Corners', one of the most sacred places of the Native American Navajo, Hopi, Ute and Zuni Nations (see page 127).

This is a profoundly transformative eclipse, made even more significant because the Sun and Moon are conjunct with the Pleiades. This well-known cluster of stars, above Taurus, has held a significant position in world mythology throughout the ages. To the Maya, they represent the handful of maize seeds from which the original humans were born[2]. These seeds are replanted in the Earth at the beginning of each new 'Sun' cycle of 5,125 years.

The Pleiades are also perceived as the rattle of the rattlesnake, whose shadow descends the steps of the Kukulkan Pyramid of Chichen Itza (see Colour Plate 7), at sunset every March equinox – the cosmic snake returns to Earth, bringing its life-giving seeds each spring.

At midday Local Time on 20 May 2012, the Sun is exactly conjunct with the Pleiades perpendicularly above the Chichen Itza pyramid at its zenith. Exactly six months before this, on 20 November 2011, the Pleiades are visible at the zenith, over Chichen Itza at midnight. John Major Jenkins believes that this occurrence was used by the Aztecs to enable them to 'calibrate' the progress of the precessional cycle[3].

Eclipses occur when the Sun and Moon are conjunct either with the Moon's North or South Node. South Node Eclipses are predominantly concerned with releasing old, outmoded patterns, attitudes and archetypes, whereas North Node Eclipses are concerned with creating the space for new patterns to take root in the collective consciousness.

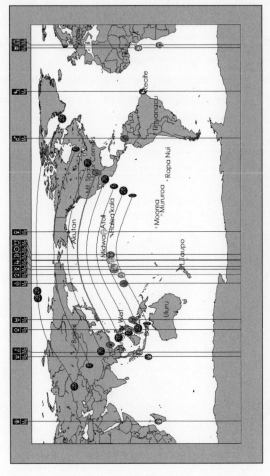

Path of Solar Annular Eclipse on 20 May 2012 with planetary Meridians at Maximum Eclipse (23:47 UT)

This is a South Node Eclipse, heralding the completion of one 'Sun' cycle, and releasing the energetic archetypes and 'thought-forms' of the last 5,125 years of the old 'Sun'. Remember that the Annular Eclipse is releasing the old energetic imprints of the mind and spirit, as the shadow traverses the atmosphere, the realm of Mind (Air). Meanwhile the Pleiades, hidden behind the eclipsing Sun, are poised to 'plant the maize seeds' for the new cycle, still as yet hidden from view.

The astrology chart of the eclipse shows two distinct patterns, linked by Neptune. The pattern involving Sun and Moon is concerned with releasing old ideals, thoughts and emotional attachments, as we search for new, practical ways

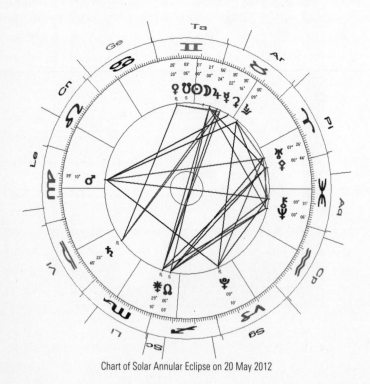

Chart of Solar Annular Eclipse on 20 May 2012

of relating and maintaining Right Relations. The other pattern is a 'Kite'; Mars holds the tail, Chiron–Neptune are at the head and Pluto and Vesta provide the wings. This pattern shows the combination of the will, heart and intuition, working together to heal the past and become fully empowered in the present. If we try to hold onto the past, Neptune will bring disillusionment, loss and a sense of things just slipping away from us. If we embrace the coming change, opening our hearts fully to receive it, then we will be carried heavenwards on the wings of the 'Kite'.

This eclipse represents the 'point of no return', on the last leg of the journey toward the December Solstice. The more we can release the emotional attachments, thoughts and ideologies that hold us back from experiencing our connection with the Oneness of all life, the smoother the remainder of the transition will be. This eclipse is our last chance to put things in order, to create Right Relations and to stand in the power of who we truly are and what we truly believe.

Total Solar Eclipse (13 November 2012)

This eclipse path, crossing the southern Pacific Ocean, is like a mirror image of the 20 May Annular Eclipse in the Northern Pacific (see page 130). The November Eclipse is Total, so its shadow touches the surface of the Earth and, as a North Node Eclipse, it brings in the New, rather than releasing the Old. So, whereas the May Eclipse was releasing old patterns and thought-forms, we now receive its mirror image, as new patterns and thought-forms are imprinted.

In the Astrology Chart, there is a pattern resembling a Kite, with its head open like a flower, to receive the new frequencies of the three planets there – Pluto, Mars and Juno.

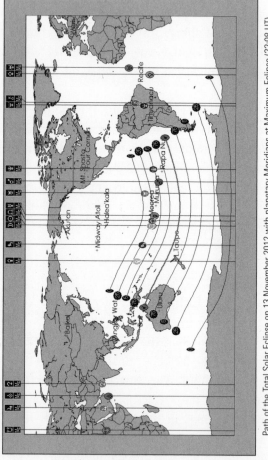

Path of the Total Solar Eclipse on 13 November 2012 with planetary Meridians at Maximum Eclipse (22:08 UT)

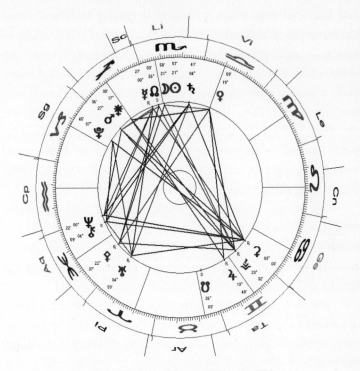

Chart of Total Solar Eclipse on 13 November 2012

The presence of Pluto and Mars at the open apex of this Kite indicates the alignment of the personal and spiritual will. More than that, Mars is flanked by Pluto and Juno, bringing us into Right Relationship with our spiritual will, our purpose, and with the universe.

Mars, the personal will, is expressing itself in complete alignment with Pluto and Juno, and is also conjunct with the Galactic Centre at 27° Sagittarius. Holding, grounding and balancing these enormous spiritual energies, at the tail of the Kite, are Ceres, Vesta and Jupiter, all retrograde. Ceres in Cancer, opposing Pluto and Mars, challenges us to release all our old emotional resistance to expressing our spiritual will in a full and balanced way. Vesta in Gemini, opposing Mars and Juno, challenges us to apply the energy of the personal will to relate to others in healthy and wholesome ways that totally honour the truth within our own hearts. Jupiter, opposing Juno, challenges us to release outmoded dualistic belief systems of either 'this is true', or 'that is true'. This opposition shows us that when we are truly in Right Relationship with ourselves, others and the world around us, then both 'this *and* that are true'. This means acknowledging and honouring our perceptions of truth, while recognizing the perspective of others.

The 'wings', which enable this kite to fly, are held by Venus on one side and Chiron–Neptune on the other. Venus in Libra is holding the whole pattern in a harmonious balance; Chiron and Neptune in Pisces bring their healing potentials into people's day-to-day lives to answer their most pressing needs.

The Sun, Moon and North Node in Scorpio bring a sense of commitment, self-reliance and self-discipline to confront our deepest emotional patterns and fears, so we can each understand the best way to move forward. The key to understanding this eclipse is that, whatever happens, it is time for us to take full responsibility for our future, and to grasp that it is our own beliefs, attitudes and deeply held inner patterns that create the circumstances of our lives – we create our own reality.

After the December 2012 Solstice, the barriers and veils that have existed within our consciousness since time immemorial will have been removed so that we can choose to live at one with the Universe and ourselves. The two eclipses over the Pacific Ocean are reconnecting us with the ancient wisdom, still held by the indigenous peoples of the Pacific. The knowledge that all of life is One is, rather ironically, now being rediscovered with the help of the vast telescopes positioned at the top of the most sacred mountain of Mauna Kea on Hawaii.

Chapter 7
DECEMBER SOLSTICE 2012

Finally, the moment we have all been waiting for... for many lifetimes. This is a moment that has not occurred for 25,626 years, the last 12,813 of which have taken us on a journey through the depths of duality, as the December Solstice Sun has traversed the southern galactic hemisphere.

The world's mythologies speak of a long distant 'Golden Age' when humans and gods walked together on the Earth. This was in the time before the Solstice Sun began its descent into the southern Galactic Hemisphere. In world myths the beginning of this descent has been remembered as a Great Flood of Noah, of Atlantis, of the Greek Deucalion, and many other versions worldwide. This Great Flood occurred at the beginning of the last Great Age of Leo, around 11,000 BCE, approximately 13,000 years ago. This was around the time when the last great Ice Age is considered to have ended, with the melting of the vast ice cap raising ocean levels and causing widespread, global flooding.

Now, as we approach the opposite point in the cycle of the Galactic Great Year, at the beginning of the Age of Aquarius, we begin to re-emerge symbolically and literally back into the Galactic Light. This may be a gradual reawakening for some, a sudden reawakening for others; for many it may be a long time before they fully awaken to the potentials that are now becoming available to every living human on the planet. It is like a great tide of change that will carry us all along. The more people awaken, the easier it will be for others to awaken. If you sit in a room on your own to meditate, it can be difficult and the mind can become easily distracted; whereas if you sit in a room with 20 other people who are all maintaining the same focus, then it becomes easier; if you are in a room with 200 focused people, then it becomes easier still. If you live on a planet with 200,000, or even 2 million spiritually focused people, then the possibilities for awakening increase exponentially.

To appreciate what the 21 December 2012 Solstice means for us individually, we need to look at the astrology for that time, both from the Earth's (geocentric) and the Sun's (heliocentric) perspective. In the following chapters we explore what this means for each person, according to their individual Sun sign.

The Astrology of the 2012 Solstice

At first glance, the geocentric Chart (see Colour Plate 16) does not appear to be anything special. It shows what needs to be learned from the level of the ego and personality. It is the Sun-centred, heliocentric chart that reveals the true spiritual potentials that emerge into human consciousness on 21 December 2012.

Geocentric Chart (21 December 2012)

In the geocentric chart, the Sun is exactly conjunct with Juno, and is within 9° orb of Pluto. The Sun's conjunction with Juno is crucial. We have seen throughout that Juno represents the principle of Right Relations. One of Juno's most important qualities is 'remembering': why we came here; why we incarnated on the Earth at this particularly powerful time. We saw earlier that Juno reminds us of our 'soul contracts', the agreements or spiritual 'tasks' that our soul has undertaken to fulfil in this lifetime. As the Sun emerges with Juno, out of the depths of Earth's Galactic Winter, it brings our soul's awareness of our spiritual purpose into the Light.

We become more fully aware of what this means for us after the Sun becomes exactly conjunct with Pluto on 30 December 2012, and Juno becomes exactly conjunct with Pluto on 14 January 2013. The Sun and Juno are in opposition to retrograde Ceres, at the end of Gemini; this should create a deepening sense that our most important relationship is with Mother Earth.

In the West we have grown up in cultures that do not appreciate the significance of this relationship; we have learned that family, or our immediate loved ones, provide our most important relationships. Without the support and nourishment from the Earth, however, we would not exist at all, nor would any of our other relationships. This may seem so obvious, yet it is a fundamental fact all too easily missed, or taken for granted, in the cultures we have created.

In recent years, global warming and the increasing frequency of natural disasters have, ever so painfully slowly, been reminding us of our total dependence on Mother Earth; she is now shouting at us so loudly, insistently and frequently that we can no longer afford to ignore her. Collectively, we have begun to act on this awareness, although for many this is still motivated by the desire to maintain a lifestyle similar to the one that created the problem. This lifestyle, which has lost any real understanding of our intimate relationship with the Earth, has only truly existed since the Industrial Revolution. Before then, we understood our dependence on Nature; since then, we have learned to exploit Her ever more ruthlessly. It is sobering to visit the home of the Industrial Revolution at Ironbridge in Shropshire, and see how beautifully the bridge now blends into the natural environment. We could learn much by contemplating this.

None of this means, however, that we need to return to pre-industrial ways of living. We can take forward the accumulated wisdom and knowledge and apply it in ways that help us to return to living in communion with Mother Earth, just as the early industrialists managed to create elegant beauty within the landscape, before it escalated into industrial greed.

Ceres is at the apex of a 'Yod', also known as a 'Finger of God', or 'Projection Figure', which is completed by Mars in Capricorn and the Moon's Node in Scorpio. Ceres challenges us to use our practical ingenuity (Mars) to create a world that enables us to live in harmony with our environment, taking only what we need (Moon's Node). The Sabian symbol[1] for the degree of the Moon's Node is 'Native American Indians making camp' – a symbol that reminds us how to live in complete harmony with Nature and her cycles.

Another 'Yod' is formed between retrograde Jupiter in Gemini, with Pluto in Capricorn and Saturn in Virgo. The Sabian symbol for Jupiter's degree is 'a quiver filled with arrows'; this refers to our capacity for using our creative skills and intentions in powerful, spiritually focused ways. We need discernment to take only what is needed, always remembering to give back to the Earth what is necessary to maintain balance.

Ceres, Jupiter and Vesta are all retrograde, and urge us to take time to reflect, using the wisdom of the intuitive mind and heart to really understand the effects that we have on the Earth. By damaging her, we damage ourselves, as surely as if we were sitting on the branch that we were cutting from the tree. What is so astonishing is that we have continued to behave for so long in ways that are so foolishly unsustainable; if it were not so serious, this would be almost comical to an outside observer from another planet.

Jupiter is in opposition to Venus in Sagittarius, reminding us that Love is the unifying principle behind everything. It is there to be expressed in *every single situation in which we find ourselves*, not just between lovers, partners, family and friends. Knowing that our most important relationship is with the Earth and that everything we do affects the Earth in some way, it is clear that *everything* we do needs to be done with loving intent. Jupiter and Mercury in opposition bring the need to apply foresight and vision, so that we can perceive the possible outcomes of our plans, and accept that we must take full responsibility if we do not act in a carefully considered and loving manner.

Chiron and Neptune remain close to each other, holding the possibility for us to receive the healing qualities of Unconditional Love. Chiron forms a T-square pattern with Jupiter and Venus, helping us to see that *all* of our decisions need to be based in Love – not just some of them, when it suits us, but all of them in every moment.

Pallas Athene is making a similar T-square with Ceres and the Sun–Juno conjunction. Pallas is helping our intuitive mind to know, in an instant, what it means to act in Right Relation with others and the Earth, at all times. Pallas close to Uranus brings spontaneity to our reactions and reminds us that we should always ask our higher intuitive mind what constitutes Right Action.

The Moon in Aries has a profound Sabian symbol associated with it: 'An Indian weaving a ceremonial blanket'. Dane Rudhyar's commentary about the meaning of this degree captures the essence of the moment at which the Sun undergoes its galactic rebirth: 'The (person) who has attained the spiritual state is figuratively robed in the Universe – and more precisely in the Milky Way, the Great White Robe of interwoven stars. This is the ultimate kind of weaving... implied is the profound fact that every individual has as (their) ultimate conscious task the weaving of the "immortal body", the Gnostic Robe of Glory.' [2]

Heliocentric Chart for 2012 Solstice

The heliocentric chart (see Colour Plate 17) shows the highest possibilities that we can aspire toward. It reveals qualities of the soul and spirit, aligned with the Divine order of the Cosmos, whereas the geocentric chart shows how we are likely to respond to these new energies at the ego and personality level. Because the heliocentric chart shows the Solar System from the Sun's perspective, the pattern of planets differs from our Earthly perspective.

The heliocentric chart for the December 2012 Solstice reveals the new spiritual impulse that is emerging into the Light. Pluto and Juno are again conjunct, forming the apex of a 'Kite' pattern. When considering heliocentric charts it is more relevant to look at the planets' positions in the Sidereal Zodiac of constellations, rather than the Tropical Zodiac used in the geocentric chart (see Chapter 2)

Pluto is in the constellation of Sagittarius, and Juno in Ophiuchus, more specifically in the tail of the serpent (Serpens) held by Ophiuchus and linking into the Galactic Equator.

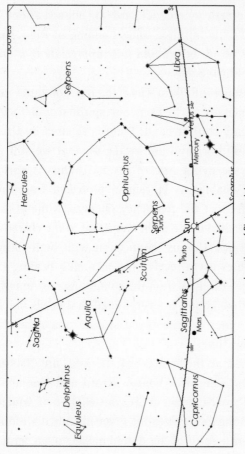

Locations of Pluto and Juno
Image Produced by Chris Marriott's SkyMap Pro

As Juno draws in the spiritual understanding of Right Relationship from the galactic plane of spiritual consciousness, this becomes grounded through Juno's opposition to the Earth and Ceres at the tail of the Kite, both in the constellation of Taurus. The close conjunction of Earth and Ceres means that the physical and etheric (energetic) Earth are aligned as one, so that we can receive the intuitive understanding of Right Relations into all levels of our being, *and fully appreciate that the Earth is a living, sentient being.*

The presence of Pluto close to, but not quite conjunct with Juno, enables us to keep our spiritual will focused on the evolutionary shift at hand; Pluto is squared by Uranus (in Pisces), keeping our intuition awake to what we still need to release from the dying Age of Pisces. Uranus is poised in a position that enables us to remain protected from the more damaging effects of the frequency changes, while at the same time allowing us to move with, and adapt to the changing flow of these energies. Uranus' connection with both Chiron and Mercury enables us to receive the incoming healing energies and nascent possibilities from the coming Age of Aquarius, and at the same time attend to every detail that needs our focused attention, in order to understand and negotiate the changing currents of this time.

Positioned at the 'wings' of the kite, are Neptune and Chiron on one side, with Venus, Saturn and Mercury on the other. Chiron and Neptune, in the constellation of Aquarius, are opening us to the flow of healing grace and unconditional love, allowing the true spirit of the Aquarian Age to cut through any remaining mental or emotional attachments to the archetypes and paradigms of the old Piscean Age.

Venus conjunct Saturn, in the constellation of Virgo, bring the spiritual discernment needed to release our deepest emotional (Venus) and physical (Saturn) attachments. Mercury, conjunct Saturn and Venus, is in the constellation of Libra, bringing clear balanced thinking into the equation. These three, so closely conjunct in the heliocentric chart, bring the possibility for a harmonious and complete integration between body, emotions and mind.

Pallas Athene, in the constellation of Pisces, makes a harmonious pattern with Mars (in Capricorn) and Jupiter and Vesta (in Taurus). Mars, Jupiter and Vesta are bringing the will, imagination and inner heart into alignment so that they can be applied in ways that produce practical solutions to the changing energies. Pallas is ensuring the balanced expression of these qualities, assisting Uranus in enabling us to release our attachments to the old ways of expressing these. She is being constantly vigilant and watchful. Positioned in the space below Pisces, between the constellations of Cetus and Aquarius, she must use her intuitive knowing to discern the difference between the truly Aquarian spiritual impulses of the coming Age, and the deep unconscious fears, attachments, or wishful thinking, created by the decaying frequencies and emotional dregs of the Piscean Age. By helping us to maintain a calm, detached attitude, Pallas can provide a point of stillness for us, in the midst of the many activities going on within us and around us.

How 2012 Affects You

In the following chapters we will explore what the coming changes are likely to mean for each of the 12 zodiac signs. Inevitably this will involve generalizations, as each person's astrology chart is unique to them, and shows complex relationships between *all* of the planets. There is no substitute for a personal in-depth astrology reading for those who want to explore the full extent of what these changes mean.

These chapters give an overview that should help you to gain a general understanding of the types of challenges that may lie ahead and the inner attitudes and awareness that may be helpful in negotiating your personal journey through them.

We saw in Chapter 3 that the Sun sign can indicate the inner qualities that we need to cultivate and develop in order to maintain a healthy and happy heart and spirit.

This is crucial to the unfolding changes, as we all need to embrace a more heart-centred, spirit-centred approach to life, others and the world, if we are to continue to maintain any reasonable quality of life and balanced relationship with our Mother Earth.

The Tropical and Sidereal Zodiacs

Each sign is described in relation to the qualities of its Tropical Zodiac position and its underlying Sidereal Zodiac constellation. The importance of understanding the differences between these two zodiacs was outlined in Chapter 2; it might be worth briefly revisiting this, before proceeding to the next chapter.

As we move through and beyond 2012, we will all need to adjust to, and integrate the higher frequencies of the Sidereal Zodiac; these enable the true resonance of our Spirit to manifest through our personality structure, as defined by the Tropical Zodiac sign. To enable this, it will be necessary to release inner attitudes, beliefs, fears and negative attachments that block or inhibit the expression of our spiritual self.

The more we can embrace the spiritual qualities of our Sidereal Zodiac sign, the easier this process will be for us. From the personality level of the ego and the critical mind, this may sometimes seem like an impossible task. But with the attitude of an open, loving and trusting heart, the power of our spirit can shine through and dissolve many of the perceived obstacles in our path, which are merely the illusions of the ego-mind.

Bear in mind that, apart from your Sun sign, you will have some planets in other zodiac signs. It is suggested that first you should read the section on your Tropical Zodiac Sun sign (Aries, Taurus, Gemini, etc), where you will also find information about its corresponding Sidereal Zodiac qualities.

Then, particularly if you know in which zodiac signs you have other planets, it is worth reading about these, too. In any event, reading about all the signs will help to gain an overall appreciation of what the changes mean for you.

CHAPTER 8

HOW 2012 AFFECTS FIRE SIGNS: ARIES, LEO, SAGITTARIUS

Fire is the elemental energy behind our impulses of creativity, passion, intuition, spontaneity, love, warmth, joy and enthusiasm for life. It can be wild and unpredictable, or it can burn with a constancy and intensity that seems to know no limits. Fire connects us directly to the creative power of the life force and the spirit. Fire sign people are direct and honest; they thrive on expressing their light and the innermost truth of their being; they may become depressed if unable to express their natural creativity and passion for life. Wherever we have planets in Fire signs, these need to be lived with passion and joy in order to fulfil their true potential.

Tropical Aries = Sidereal Pisces

20 March–19 April

For Aries, 2012 is a wake-up call for the personality to go beyond its headstrong need for independence or wilfully following desires. The fiery passion of their emotions needs to be tempered by the soothing waters of Sidereal Pisces; this can then bring the awareness that true independence of spirit is only achieved when we learn to move with the flow of life, and align our feelings with the needs and purpose of the greater whole. Sidereal Pisces is awakening Fiery Aries to the need for self-sacrifice; to apply their warrior-like qualities toward fighting for a cause, combining the inner truth of their being with a sense of justice toward others and the world in general.

Aries is being challenged, like never before, to let go of personal attachments to material things, to money or to acting from any need to 'prove themselves'. The proof of their inner worth will come from acting with nobility and passion for the common good, training their energies on a deep sense of purpose, and acknowledging their innate qualities of leadership. Some will manifest this in small ways in their immediate surroundings, family or work; others will recognize a larger need, and will take courage to step forward and meet the challenges required.

Aries needs to understand how to avoid getting caught in day-to-day dramas, intrigues, gossip and small-mindedness, or reacting to the slightest hurt or slight. If they can let down their guard and allow themselves to experience the vulnerability of the heart, knowing that they have the inner strength to deal with whatever comes their way, then they can embrace the wider view of life, understanding the personal contribution they can make within the context of the larger whole. This means moving away from Aries' accustomed way of thinking about themselves and their needs; moving away from 'me' consciousness to an awareness of 'me as part of the whole'. This requires a level of detachment and equanimity of the heart. It can be challenging for Aries to stand back and see themselves and their behaviour objectively, with their feet planted firmly on the ground, fully present in the here and now.

Mars is the ruler of Aries and, at the personality level, this gives a strong tendency for 'fight or flight', to act now and think later, or if everything just feels too emotionally or physically unsafe, then to just 'get the hell out of here'. The impulses and energies of 2012 are challenging Aries to stand their ground without the need for fight *or* flight; when Aries becomes centred in the heart and not the will, then it can use its strength of will to stay present in each moment and not react according to old emotional patterns or past hurts, and to feel the support from the Earth beneath the feet. The lesson for Aries is to remain rooted and calm; when the going gets tough, to breathe and to take the time to see the larger picture of which they are an integral part.

So how does Aries learn to move the attention from the will (in the belly) up to the heart? Aries, like all the Fire signs, is quick – this is often because they do not naturally have the patience to be otherwise! All that it takes, however, when there is the urge to act compulsively or rashly, is to stop and draw breath, relax the diaphragm and breathe up from the belly and into the heart, and allow the heart to open and expand. As the heart opens calmly to perceive the true needs of the situation, it remains rooted in the will, through the breath. This relationship of heart and will is the essence of the relationship between the Fire and Water of Tropical Aries and Sidereal Pisces. Water restrains the excesses of Aries' fiery nature, so that when triggered, the energy in the body does not all rush up to the head, causing Aries to act in ways they may later regret.

The build-up to 2012 challenges Aries to examine their emotional reaction patterns and the way that they structure their emotional lives, partnerships and business relationships, and also what they take into their bodies through food and drink. Saturn requires Ariens to develop a deep level of discernment about everything and everyone that they connect to, in deep, meaningful or intimate ways. This represents the most essential aspect of what needs to heal for Aries.

If Ariens are experiencing struggle, obstacles or blocks to their progress, particularly in the areas of emotional commitments and partnerships, then it will be because, at some deep level, they are not being true to the essence of who they are. They may not be willing to open up to the healing possibilities offered by awakening to their spiritual nature, listening to the promptings of their inner voice and what it is telling them they need to be doing with their lives.

Meanwhile, 2012 demands that we all remain present in each moment and live it to its fullest, with all our heart, mind and will. If Ariens are not doing this, then they may feel huge levels of frustration, self-doubt, or loss of confidence. It is not enough to push ahead regardless and trust that everything will be OK. If there are unresolved issues needing to be healed, then it is important to focus attention with courage, on what most needs to heal within them. Whatever the individual circumstances, at its root, this will be concerned with understanding their place in the Universe. Ariens must surrender the ego's need to be fully in control at all times, in order to realize that the Universe is supporting them and answering their needs. If they can just become still and observe themselves with calm inner detachment, then they will be able to tap into the deepest levels of their creative resources. This may sound simple, but for Aries it can bring the greatest of challenges.

Aries is learning inner spiritual 'poise'; how to remain fully alert, and ready for the moment of action, but only when the prompting to act springs from their inner knowing. This is the difference between conscious action and unconscious re-action. When Ariens are able to master this skill, then they will act appropriately with 'Right Action' and these actions will have great power.

Tropical Leo = Sidereal Cancer & Leo

22–23 July–22 August

The first half of Tropical Leo is currently aligned with the constellation of Cancer; the last half is aligned with the constellation of Leo. So Leo's date of birth will indicate whether they are more influenced by the constellation of Cancer or Leo. Those born between 22 July and 7 August will have the underlying watery influence of Cancer; those born from 8 and 22 August will have more of the underlying fiery influence of Leo.

Leo is ruled by the Sun and Cancer is ruled by the Moon, so, those born in the first half of Leo are learning to balance the fiery radiance of the Sun with the more reflective, sensitive qualities of the Moon. Those born in the last half of Leo are fire within fire – they are learning to balance the fiery extraverted qualities of Leo with the deep radiance of their inner spiritual, creative fire.

The principal challenge that 2012 brings for Leos is how to apply their creativity in practical ways toward the service of others. Leos love to 'shine' and be the centre of attention; now, they are being required to 'shine', not just for themselves but in service to the greater whole. This requires Leos to acknowledge their ability to attract others to them by their light and radiance, and create a dramatic impact in the world around them. If this is just used to feed Leo's ego, or to compensate for inner feelings of hurt or inadequacy, then it is likely that their sensitive inner core will feel misunderstood or rejected – behind many Leos' radiant exterior, there is the deep watery sensitivity of Cancer, at their core.

If Leo can step into 'selfless mode', then the rewards and recognition that follow will surpass expectations. This is rather like Alice through the looking glass, needing to walk in the opposite direction to where she wants to be. More than ever, Leos are being challenged to realize that their creativity comes not from them, but *through* them, their creative abilities and their sense of self being drawn from the energy of the Sun. As the Sun aligns with the Galactic Centre at December Solstice, this can bring a deep understanding of the unlimited potentials, and creative possibilities, that become available when the ego is surrendered to the will of the spiritual self.

The spiritual purpose of Leos at this time is to become as firmly rooted and grounded as possible; to surround themselves with their true 'spiritual family', and to create the best possible environment for their creative talents to thrive. When Leos are settled and happy then spontaneous creativity will follow; when Leos are living and working in the right place, then they will meet the right people, and make all the right connections needed to fulfil their creative possibilities. At this time, understanding the principle of true service to others is crucial. The Sun shines, not just for its own benefit of Being, but in order to sustain the movements of all the planets and other bodies in the Solar System, some orbiting at unimaginable distances from it. We have seen how the Sun and planets are created from the same primordial substance. It is important now for Leos to understand that there is no separation between themselves and others, and that their creativity is their gift to others.

The message for Leos is to become aware of the repercussions and influence that they can have, not just in their immediate environment but often in ways that they cannot possibly anticipate. The more that creative action is undertaken for its own sake, the more pure an expression it will be of that person's spirit, and the further-reaching its effects and influence.

Leos are being asked to develop true independence of spirit and in doing this, to manifest more and more of their unique individuality and genius. This is about stepping beyond the fear of being hurt or unappreciated; it is about Leos knowing their inner worth in a genuine, deep yet humble way, without hiding their light or diminishing its power and brilliance in any way. When we know our true inner worth, without needing it to be constantly reflected back to us, then our thoughts, feelings and actions can have a compelling influence on others, because they recognize that Leo is expressing an aspect of the creative source that lies within us all.

When Leos are not dependent on the approval or praise of others, they are free to express themselves with the innocence of a child. Leos need this level of emotional freedom to be true to themselves. At this time, it is essential for Leos to let go of limiting beliefs about themselves, to let go of reaction patterns that stem from childhood insecurities or perceived emotional rejection. It is essential for Leos to be able to live fully in the moment. If they are harbouring old fears or memories of past hurts, then that will inhibit their capacity for spontaneous reaction to their surroundings; it is Alice through the looking glass again. By cultivating emotional independence, Leos become free to express their true emotional selves, and therefore receive all the love, warmth and recognition that they crave and need.

For Leo, the deepest healing of 2012 is to understand how to let go of attachment to the values, judgments, opinions or limited perceptions of others. Holding onto these will only cause energy loss and dissipation of their talents; letting go will open them up to receive the healing potentials of the Universe, enabling it to flow into their consciousness and bringing Leos the certainty of inner knowing that they are truly a 'Child of the Universe'.

Tropical Sagittarius = Sidereal Scorpio & Ophiuchus

21 November–21 December

As with Leo, Tropical Sagittarius spans two constellations – Scorpio and Ophiuchus. From 21 to 30 November it receives the underlying and deep watery influence of Scorpio. From 1 to 21 December it receives the influence of Ophiuchus, which is not one of the traditional zodiac signs, and so does not have an associated element. It spans the Ecliptic and the Galactic Equator, suggesting that it is attributable to Ether, or the life force. This corresponds to the Wood element in the Chinese system; the Galactic Equator is referred to in different mythologies as the 'World Tree', or 'Cosmic Tree'. In Mayan cosmology, this is the *wakah-chan,* or 'raised-up sky', the central axis of the Cosmos[1]. So the fire of Tropical Sagittarius is fed by the deep waters of Scorpio or the energy of the Life Force itself, emanating from the Galactic Centre.

It may seem strange to think of water as generating fire, but this principle is well understood in Chinese Medicine. It is found in the *ming men*, the 'fire of vitality' that resides deep in the belly, in front of and just below the kidneys. The kidneys (water) contain our vital ancestral and constitutional essence (*jing*). It is their ability to filter and purify the blood that maintains a healthy heart (fire) and life force (qi).

In a similar way the deep and intense energy of Scorpio serves to test and purify the emotional nature, so that we can learn to rise above the emotional attachments of the desires that hold us bound to the material world; when we release ourselves from these deep emotional attachments, then the consciousness-raising and healing energies of Ophiuchus act through Sagittarius, enabling us to soar heavenwards and reclaim our spiritual birthright.

As we approach 2012, Sagittarians are being challenged to be true to their essence. The changing energies are heightening their sensitivity, bringing ever more demanding challenges in their dealings with the apparent 'follies' of the world. Sagittarians' inner attunement (conscious or unconscious) to the energies of the Galaxy, are making them acutely aware of all that is wrong in the world – socially, culturally, emotionally and environmentally. There may be an overwhelming urge to escape, but it is important to realize that this urge can only be met if that 'escape' is by way of forging a deep and lasting relationship with their inner spiritual essence. Now is the time for Sagittarians to remain 'in the world, but not of the world'.

Sagittarius is ruled by Jupiter, enabling us to reach up to heaven with the imagination and higher mind, at the same time remaining in touch with the material world through all the senses. This ability to perceive and feel both the spiritual and physical reality simultaneously gives Sagittarians a complete and whole perception of life. This also brings the knowledge that our perceptions of the physical world are incomplete, or illusory, unless we also understand the essential nature of the spiritual world.

If Sagittarians get caught up in battling against all the wrongs of the world, they end up exhausted and defeated, because there will always be something else to tackle. It is essential for Sagittarians, at this time, to understand the nature of their psychological Shadow. There will be a strong tendency to 'project' their unresolved inner conflicts out into the world, so that they may end up fighting shadows, or like Don Quixote, 'tilting against windmills', allowing their imaginations to turn them into giants. The more power Sagittarius invests in projecting their inner fears or conflicts onto outside situations, the more powerless they will feel.

When they take a step back and view the world with equanimity, however, they will come back into Right Relationship with their core values and draw their strength, stability and constancy from within. For Sagittarius, the task is to move into stillness and descend into the quiet depths of their being; then to allow the folly and chaos of the outside world to whirl like a hurricane around them, while they remain in the still eye of the storm, moving with the changing and volatile energies, without losing their centre. The minute they lose centre, they will become caught up in the maelstrom; only by remaining still themselves can they connect with the profound stillness emanating from the centre of the Galaxy. This can connect them to an inner peace, passing all understanding.

It requires self-discipline and ruthless honesty with themselves to own their reactions to what they see happening around them. There is a fine line between discerning what is an appropriate emotional response to all the folly and chaos around and what is a response that is just being amplified by their own unresolved emotional issues.

Sagittarius (like all Fire signs) has an innate sense of knowing what is 'right'; the key is to discern the difference between what is right for them and what is right for the world at large; what is true for them, and what may be true for others. The perception of Truth depends on your perspective; the higher you ascend the mountain, the more you are able to perceive the totality of the view below. But even then you may not fully perceive the larger pattern behind the way that things are unfolding. By remaining true to their core values, no matter what the cost, Sagittarians will be able to move forward, one step at a time – this can be a challenge for Sagittarians, who would prefer to have already arrived at their goal, so that they can make plans for reaching the next one!

It is really important for Sagittarians not to become distracted by reaching their objective; what is important is living the journey fully in every moment, and ensuring that they are consciously aware of the effects that their actions are having on others and on the world around them. From a place of inner stillness, their challenge is to express congruent thoughts, feelings and body language in all dealings with others; the relationship with those around them is crucial to their own wellbeing. When they are not in Right Relationship with their own still centre and with others, then the reactions from the world around them can be instant and extreme.

This is a challenging time for Sagittarians, as they are the ones through whom (consciously or unconsciously) the energies of the Galactic Centre are flowing most strongly. They, more than anyone, have direct access to the creative energies behind the turbulent times through which we are passing. Therefore, to negotiate these powerful energies, it is essential for Sagittarians to remain grounded and in touch with the Earth, to maintain a still, calm emotional equilibrium, and to swiftly confront their emotional responses, so that they can remain as clear 'vessels' through which these sublime frequencies can flow.

For the rest of us, we would do well to listen carefully to what our Sagittarian brothers and sisters are telling us; to listen for the essence and inner truth behind what they are saying and doing, while still using our discernment. They are in touch with something profound and potentially transformative, which can help to point us all in the right direction for negotiating the changing currents of this time.

CHAPTER 9
HOW 2012 AFFECTS EARTH SIGNS: TAURUS, VIRGO, CAPRICORN

The Earth element is concerned with stability, security, practicality and being in touch with the senses. Earth is slow, pragmatic and methodical. It may sometimes get 'bogged down' in the practicalities of life, at the expense of a more inspired approach to life. However, this element is also the means through which our spirit becomes fully present in the body. All too often our spirit fails to fully anchor into the body; this may be due to birth trauma; it may stem from the past-life memory of a difficult life, or painful death; it may stem from unconscious resistance to the tasks that our soul has chosen to undertake, or it may simply be a lack of knowing how to fully connect with the physical plane. Earth teaches us to appreciate the physical, the beauty of the world and the sense of being alive and fully embodied. Above all, Earth teaches us what is needed in order to nurture our bodies, emotions, mind and spirit.

Tropical Taurus = Sidereal Aries & Taurus

21 April–21 May

The first three-quarters of Tropical Taurus span the constellation of Aries, and the last quarter receives the influence of the stars of Taurus. So, from 21 April to 14 May, the earthy energy of Taurus is underpinned by the fiery energy from the stars of Aries. From 15 to 21 May, Tropical Taurus receives the influence of the constellation of Taurus itself, linking the physical and spiritual aspects of this sign.

Though an Earth element sign, many regard Taurus the Bull as potentially the most spiritual of all signs, as it carries the possibility of fully incarnating all of one's potentials. The stars that form the horns of the Bull reach out to touch the Galactic Equator near its point of intersection with the Ecliptic (see page 159), on the opposite side of the zodiac from where Ophiuchus/Scorpio intersects the Galactic Equator (see Chapter 4).

This is one of the reasons why bull cults have persisted in so many cultures and with such importance, over millennia; the worship, or more often the slaying, of the bull, is perceived as a means of 'stepping off' the path of reincarnation (the Ecliptic), and 'stepping onto' the path leading back to the Divine (the Galactic Equator). Ophiuchus, Scorpio and Sagittarius are the gatekeepers at one end of the Milky Way, while Taurus, the Pleiades and Gemini are the gatekeepers at the other end. To the Mayans, the Pleiades were perceived as the seeds of maize that created the first humans, and recreate them at the beginning of each new 'Sun' cycle of 5125¼ years. The Pleiades were used to accurately calibrate the end of the Long Count (precessional) calendar cycle. Those born between 20 and 22 May have their Sun exactly conjunct with the Pleiades, so are likely to be particularly attuned to the power of these creator gods.

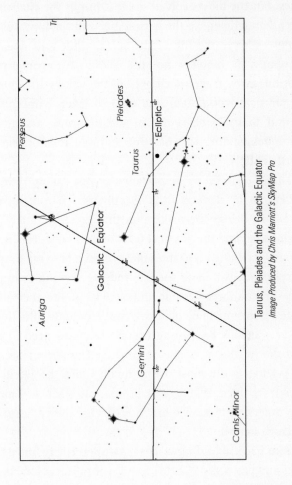

Taurus, Pleiades and the Galactic Equator
Image Produced by Chris Marriott's SkyMap Pro

For Taureans, the Moon's South Node, positioned in Taurus in December 2012, brings the challenge to release old patterns of attachment to the past. This is not just about releasing the attachments of this lifetime, but from many lifetimes. For the most evolved souls, it brings the challenge to release *all* attachment to the personality and the physical body and fully embrace the life of the spirit, while still remaining in the body. It requires nothing short of a complete re-orientation, away from attachment to the values and comforts of the physical world. Taureans need to listen with complete conviction to the inner voice of the intuition, and to their innate understanding of what true spiritual relationship with the Earth entails.

Taurus enables us to experience the many levels of enjoyment to be derived from the physical world, in all its beauty; 2012 brings the realization that there are many more dimensions beyond the physical level of existence. This may be a gradually dawning realization that has been brewing for years, or it may come as a more sudden, rude awakening as physical security or comforts become threatened by the increasingly unstable environmental, political and economic situation. In whatever way this awakening occurs, Taureans need to move beyond the fulfilment of the personal self as their main goal, and ask what is the most useful quality that the world now requires from them; this may be in terms of what they have to offer to others, or it may be in terms of what they have to offer to the Earth herself.

As an Earth sign, Taurus' basic nature is finely tuned to the rhythms and patterns of Mother Earth. The physical attachments of the ego-self are simply a distraction and distortion of this much deeper, more fundamental quality. When Taureans listen long and deep enough to their inner voice, they may hear the voice of the Earth speaking to them; more importantly, they feel it resonating in every cell of their bodies. Comfort, or discomfort, felt in the physical body tells Taureans whether they are on the right track in any given moment. When something needs to change, there will be physical discomfort; when things are right then there will be a sense of inner and outer harmony and physical ease.

We have seen that Taurus is one of the 'gatekeepers' to the Milky Way Galaxy. Every Taurean has the potential to enable the creativity of the Divine Cosmic Mother to manifest in their daily lives, though clearly not every Taurean will choose to realize this potential.

Taurus is ruled by Venus, goddess of love and beauty and so, at this time, every Taurean has the opportunity to create beauty in all aspects of their lives, by calling in the energy of Love. This will show them how to infuse everything they create with loving intent, in order to bring transformation into their own lives and the lives of those around them.

This also means 'remembering' how to honour the Earth as a living being, acknowledging our share of responsibility for her and treating her as if she were our most cherished companion, lover and friend. For some that responsibility may extend just as far as the boundaries of their home and garden; for others it may extend across the country, or toward protecting a particular species, or environment, or across the whole world.

Wherever Taureans perceive a need and are deeply affected by that need at a feeling level, it is important to realize that they are being called to do something to make a difference. The key is to realize that when they have a strong emotional response to a particular situation, they have a responsibility to act on that. The moment they decide to act, all the power and assistance needed to be effective and make a difference will flow to them. Once their actions gain momentum, there will be no stopping them until they reach their goal or objective. The more they communicate their deepest beliefs and convictions to others, the more others will be inspired to act.

2012 challenges Taureans to make an about turn in their core values around security. This means letting go of old beliefs about what they need to feel secure, being open to the values of others, and realising that true security comes from being in Right Relationship with the world around them, in an open-hearted, giving and generous way. The more Taureans try to 'hold on' at this time, the more their security is likely to feel threatened; they more they can 'let go and let flow', the more the security they seek will come naturally toward them.

The most profound level of security for Taureans comes when they look within and find their deep connection with Mother Earth. Now is the time to fully realize that they are children of the Earth, and when they acknowledge and honour that fundamental relationship, then Mother Earth will take care of all their needs, but in her own way and in her own time – the key is to trust and know that you are loved for who you are, not for what you have or what you do.

Tropical Virgo = Sidereal Leo & Virgo

23 August–22 September

Most of Tropical Virgo spans the constellation of Leo, so Virgos born between 22/23 August and 16 September receive the fiery influence of Leo's stars; those born between the 17 and 22/23 September receive the more earthy influence from the stars of Virgo.

Virgo is 'mutable', transformative Earth, so that the spiritual influence of Fire coming from the constellation of Leo is similar to the action of a kiln upon the earthly substance of Virgo. At an intuitive level, Virgos understand that the spiritual influence of Leo's fire is continually transforming them at physical and personality levels, 'fixing' the qualities that they have developed, in much the same way that a potter's pot only remains malleable up to the point when it is placed in the kiln. This is partly why Virgos are motivated by the need to create perfection in all they do.

Those born in the last few degrees of the sign have the more congruent influence of Earth emanating from the stars of Virgo. This is no less challenging, however, since these Virgos will be programmed to live up to more spiritual ideals of perfection; these ideals are embodied, in the most exalted expressions of human perfection, in such spiritual figures as Isis and Mother Mary. These archetypes of the 'Virgin Goddess' refer to their inner purity and emotional self-containment; they represent the potential within all women to be whole, in and of themselves, without any dependency on another (male or female) to feel complete.

The congruency of the stars of Virgo with the last few degrees of Tropical Zodiac Virgo shows the integration that is possible for some Virgos; the understanding that they are complete and perfect in themselves, and having a direct connection with the pure creative power of the Goddess. That power is the essence of Virgo's ability to create, to give birth to other beings, ideas, projects – in short, to create ever more perfection in the world around them.

For male Virgos, the challenge is to connect with the positive aspects of the creative power of the feminine, and to understand their relationship with this creative force. Virgo's gift is their ability to perceive the intricate interconnections between the many aspects of the rich tapestry of Life, and to understand the importance of detail.

Virgo is ruled by Mercury, which enables the mind to understand the most intricate and minute details of how the Universe and all Life within it weaves and interacts. Virgos have a fine balancing act to perform; on the one hand, they must develop a finely tuned discerning, analytical mind, in order to perceive the perfection that exists within every aspect of the Universe; on the other hand, they need to develop a deep connection with the creative power of the Universal Mother principle.

If they misunderstand some of the detail, then they will not see the perfection and will believe that they have to intervene in some way to make it 'more perfect'. The perfection of the Universe was well understood by the ancient Chinese sage Lao-Tzu and his Taoist followers; he also knew that if you interfere, or try to change that perfection because you do not understand it, you inevitably end up ruining it[1].

Conversely, if Virgo blindly follows and trusts that 'everything is perfect', without understanding what is needed to sustain that perfection, or more correctly to remain in Right Relationship with that perfection, then they will not fulfil their natural role in the universe. Virgos need to be alert to all the details going on around then, so that they can always respond in appropriate ways, without interfering.

For Virgos, the key to negotiating the changes of 2012 lies in letting go of rigid belief systems about how things 'should' be, or how to make the world more perfect by insisting on their own ideas of perfection. Instead Virgo is challenged to recognize that the world is unfolding perfectly, and that they need to respond to individual needs in practical, down-to-earth ways.

In order for Virgos to act appropriately in different situations and remain in 'Right Relationship', it may become increasingly necessary to go against their most deeply cherished beliefs. This is a time for 'getting real' and not hanging on to ideals of achieving some far-off goal of perfection; the time is now, and it is perfect now – all Virgo needs to do is recognize that. 'But, but, but...' says the Virgo mind as it seeks to make everything fit together neatly, conforming to its limited perceptions of perfection. As we look around at the apparent chaos being generated by the profound changes taking place, it can be hard to understand that everything is evolving in perfect order.

One of the professions often associated with Virgo is nursing. Virgos' insight and attention to detail can bring the understanding of what is needed to 'nurse' themselves and others back to a more healthy relationship with the natural world. This is a highly creative time for Virgos, brimming with possibilities and potentials. One of the most creative areas is adapting how they relate to others, with the changing circumstances of the time.

Virgo is acutely aware of what needs to be healed; at times this may feel overwhelming. It is also becoming clear that the old beliefs and behaviour patterns are simply not working as they used to. A new approach is needed, which requires digging deep into the root causes behind their own, and the world's, ills. This is not an easy process for Virgos, as it requires confronting and acknowledging what they may perceive to be the less than perfect aspects of their emotional Shadow. When Virgos dare to do this, they start to come back to Right Relationship with the inner power of their true creative potentials.

The key is to understand that they are co-creators with the Universe. In order to bring about positive change, the Universe needs Virgo to 'act on its behalf'. However, there is a fine line between truly acting on behalf of the Universe, as in the Buddhist practice of 'non-action', and acting from the ego's belief that it knows what is right for everyone. This is why it is essential for Virgo to constantly ask 'what is Right Action' in every instance and then to wait for the answer to come. That means allowing time for the assimilation of much information, coming in from the mind, feelings and senses, so that Virgo can get a complete picture of what is going on and what is an appropriate response.

This is a time of great potential power for Virgos; power to challenge the status quo by not conforming to habitual patterns of behaviour, once they reach an inner knowing that something is wrong and needs to change. The motivation behind such challenges should always be to heal the given situation; this can only occur when Virgo has taken the time to get to the root of what really needs to heal, and not merely by what is going on at more superficial levels. Virgos need to 'dig deep' to pull out the weeds growing within their consciousness, before they can cultivate the ground for new growth to occur.

If this is not done with the attention to detail that Virgo is so good at, then what grows next will be overwhelmed by the 'weeds' of old ideas, concepts or beliefs. Worse still, what is created may have the opposite effect to what was intended. This is a powerful time for Virgo, so it is important that they are honest with themselves and wield their power responsibly. Only then can they ensure that what they create has complete integrity, and is fully aligned with the emerging potentials of what occurs after December 2012.

Tropical Capricorn = Sidereal Sagittarius

21 December–20 January

Tropical Capricorn spans most of the constellation of Sagittarius. So, this is a time when the spiritual fire of Sagittarius can become fully grounded into human consciousness and 'anchored' into the very structure of the Earth and into our bodies.

At the 2012 December Solstice, the Sun, Juno, Pluto and Mars are all in Capricorn, making this time of great potential for spiritual rebirth and empowerment particularly significant for Capricorns. The nature and level of empowerment that is realized will be dependent on Capricorn's willingness to let go of the concerns and attachments of the ego; this is what it means to be in Right Relationship with the inner self.

Capricorn can be so driven by ambition to create a sense of inner and outer security that this letting go can be difficult. Yet, the sign of Capricorn always begins with the Winter Solstice (in the Northern Hemisphere), the time of rebirth and renewal at a personal level. In 2012 it is also a time of rebirth and renewal at a global and cosmic level, so it is essential for Capricorns to understand how to wait and how to listen to their inner voice as we approach this time.

Capricorns are being called to discover what is their service to others and to the Earth; if Capricorns already have a sense of this, now is the time to fully commit to following that path of service, letting go of any fear-based concerns for their own security or material advancement. One of the key words often used to describe Capricorn is 'responsibility'; this can often weigh heavy on Capricorns, as they can feel that they alone are responsible for their family, their business, their country, or the entire world – a heavy responsibility to assume. In whatever way Capricorns seek to be of service to the world at large, it is essential that they understand how to ask for help; this help needs to come from within, from the inner, spiritual dimensions, from their spiritual guides and helpers, as well as from without, by creating a good support network in the world around them.

Perhaps the greatest lesson for Capricorns is to overcome their resistance to creating the emotional support that they need, and learning to delegate power to others; this can be their greatest healing, as they let go of the need to be in control and learn to trust in the judgment of others. In this time of uncertainty and constantly changing goalposts, the world may feel like a very insecure and unpredictable place that can rock Capricorns to their very foundations and create high levels of emotional anxiety. The more that Capricorns are reliant on anything physical in the outside world for their sense of security, the more challenging a time this will be.

The lesson is that true support lies with their friends and support network, and in listening to their inner guidance, so long as that guidance is reliable and does not stem from a place of fear or anxiety. Capricorn the goat can have a reputation for being a bit of a loner, or for striking out on adventures that they feel others will not understand. The alternative is to 'play it safe' and stick with familiar surroundings and people, all the while harbouring that niggling feeling that maybe things would be better if they just dared to strike out to follow their dream. With Saturn as their ruling planet, the fear of failure is always present in the background of any Capricorn endeavour, and this can become undermining, debilitating or sometimes totally incapacitating.

Now is the time for Capricorns to face the fear of being vulnerable and to actively seek help and the cooperation of others. This is not something to be done indiscriminately; it begins by acknowledging that there are things that Capricorns cannot do or be on their own, and that something needs to be healed. What needs to heal is their fear of the loss of self, by surrendering to something greater than the personal self. The irony is that, while Capricorns may feel that their sense of power comes from being in control of themselves and their environment, the opposite is actually true, particularly at this most auspicious of times.

The more that Capricorns can let go of control and the sense of personal identity that brings, then the more their inner power will flow to them. For there to be true power, this must come to us in some way; it can come from the outside, from the respect and approval of others for what we do, who we are and what we have achieved; it can also come from the inside, when we move beyond the belief that the ego-self has any reality, and understand that true empowerment comes from the spirit. For balance, we need to experience power coming to us in both of these ways. If we have discovered our true inner spiritual power and are acting according to that in the world, then others will naturally recognize our integrity and support us in the expression of our power.

In order to truly wield power in the world, Capricorns need humility, but there is a fine line between humility and insecurity. Humility comes from knowing our strengths, while at the same time realizing that these qualities come through us, from our spirit and not from our ego. Insecurity comes when we do not acknowledge our strengths, so have self-doubt. The combination of power and humility can be world-changing. When Capricorns have the humility to listen to their inner voice and feelings, to ask what is right and have the know-how, self-control and power to implement that, then they will receive all the support that they need from the world around them.

As we approach the Galactic turning point of the December 2012 Solstice, Capricorns can lead the way in showing us all how to let go of the ego and surrender with humility to inner knowing. This gives access to the 'direct line' that the human personality has to the soul, that the soul has to the Spirit, and that our Individual Spirit has to the Cosmic Great Spirit. Through humble surrender, Capricorns can come into full alignment with the power of the Universe; then all things become possible for them.

CHAPTER 10
HOW 2012 AFFECTS AIR SIGNS:
GEMINI, LIBRA, AQUARIUS

Air signs are primarily concerned with the mind and how we communicate our ideas to others. Air is the realm of all thoughts, from the most lofty and profound to the most basic and mundane. Air connects us with the energetic mental blueprints, or 'thought-forms' that underpin the physical world. Air is the Breath of Life, carrying light and heat from the Sun into our bodies, and into our blood, where the sunlight (Fire), combines with oxygen (Air) moving through the blood (Water) to nourish and sustain our physical bodies (Earth).

Air is concerned with the quality of life. When air can move it remains healthy and clear. When it stagnates, then it will become stale, causing our thinking to become stuck, lacking clarity and leading to ignorance, prejudice or bigotry. Our thoughts need to be free to soar to the heights of inspiration (literally 'in-breathing'), and to explore the appropriateness and desirability of allowing them to become a reality in the world. Just because we can think something, does not necessarily mean it is a good idea to bring that thought into manifestation.

Tropical Gemini = Sidereal Taurus

21 May–21 June

The airy, inquisitive and changeable nature of Tropical Gemini is influenced by the Earthy energies of Sidereal Taurus; this combination can send Geminis on a quest to understand the physical nature of the Universe and how everything in their world is interconnected and interdependent. However, 2012 brings the realization that merely gathering information about all the component parts of the Universe is not enough of itself to understand the nature of our reality.

The three celestial bodies in Gemini at the December 2012 Solstice (Jupiter, Vesta and Ceres) are all retrograde; Geminis are being challenged to let go of negative beliefs about themselves, which perpetuate the personality's attachment to behaviour patterns that do not serve them; they are being called to explore the deeper meanings of life that can only be felt by the heart. It is also safe to say that whatever Geminis have believed about the nature of reality in the past, their perceptions about that reality are about to change in profound and unimagined ways. This is not to say that their previous perceptions were wrong, but that they now need to go to a deeper level, if they are truly to make sense of the world around them and the larger Universe.

Gemini is ruled by Mercury, which governs the functions of the rational mind, and our ability to communicate. However, it is no longer enough just to have the facts, nor even to see the connections between things; to make sense of all this information, Geminis need to integrate it at a deeper level, by making the connection between the mind and the heart. When they do this, then they can find the enduring and fundamental truths of existence that underpin the many and varied manifestations of the Universe. This is a time for exploring new ways of communicating what they have understood about the world and the Universe.

For Gemini, the exchange of ideas has always been important, but now there is a need to ask 'what does it all mean?' Geminis are acutely aware of the constantly changing nature of the world around them, and they revel in this diversity and change. Now they need to understand that the nature of the questions they ask about the world will help to determine their perception of reality. It is not so much the answer that is important, as the question that is asked. As soon as a question arises in the mind of Gemini, they should know that they already have the answer somewhere within them. This is a challenge for Geminis, as the tendency is to look for answers outside of themselves, or become so caught up in following the thread of ideas and discoveries that they can forget their original question.

2012 calls on Geminis to apply their curiosity about what is happening around them, to enable them to 'join up the dots' and see how everything is interconnected. Then they need to see their part and their responsibility within that overall pattern in order to be in Right Relationship with their environment. The time for simply observing and being fascinated by the diversity of the world is passed. Now Geminis need to be fully engaged with the world, acknowledging their unique gift of seeing the interconnections between things and people, understanding the patterns unfolding around them, and encouraging and inspiring others to do the same.

Gemini loves the freedom to 'flit' from one idea to another, from one project to another, or even from one relationship to another. Now Geminis are asked to do the hardest thing for them – to find an inner constancy of focus and purpose. This is about healing their relationship with the apparent duality of opposites in the Universe; it is about perceiving and embracing the fact that they are an intricate part of the complex, diverse patterns that they see all around them; it is about surrendering to the vastness of the Universe, and accepting that the mind alone will never make sense of it all.

What follows such surrender is the ability to gain a true understanding of their unique purpose in the world, to see the individual gifts that they bring and to use those gifts in the service of others. This takes commitment, which can be difficult for Air signs and for Geminis in particular, as it may feel that this limits their need for freedom. The commitment required here is to remain constant and focused on a goal. The challenge now is not just for mental commitment and focus, but also for emotional commitment and focus.

This is like the commitment of the seabird, hovering over the ocean waiting for the right moment to dive into the water and catch its prey. Geminis' immersion in the waters of the emotions does not need to last so long that they become overwhelmed, but it needs to be done with focus, intent and a sense of purpose, so that their emotional encounters have real and lasting meaning.

In order to be healthy and fulfilled, Geminis require rhythm in all that they do, but Gemini's changeability can at times become chaotic or random. At this time it is important for Geminis to find a natural rhythm in all aspects of their lives, and to understand that everything that is happening is part of the larger unfolding pattern. It is important to resist the urge to flit to the next thing when the going gets tough, or only focus on the things that are easy; similarly it is important not to get stuck in only focusing on the things that are difficult.

Geminis are keenly aware of the opposites and contradictions in life. The problem is that immediately a thought arises, then its opposite thought will not be far away. This can cause Gemini to lurch indecisively from one extreme to the other. In any situation, it can mean that if something is causing Gemini happiness, lurking behind that can be its opposite that can quickly make them unhappy. At this time, Geminis need to develop the attitude of the quantum physicists – to understand that their perspective, viewpoint or emotional expectations genuinely influence the outcome of every situation in which they find themselves.

As the energetic frequencies in the Solar System are speeding up, then the reaction times between the occurrence of 'this' and its opposite 'that' are becoming shorter and shorter. It can feel as if everything is becoming more volatile, in a constant state of flux. At some level, Geminis have always had a sense of the impermanence and changeable nature of the physical world, thoughts and feelings, which can arise and fall in an instant. Now, it can feel as if Geminis are being buffeted mercilessly by the changing energies around them, bringing confusion, indecision and insecurity.

The key to dealing with, and finding a rhythm to, life is for Geminis to find their 'still point' of inner equilibrium. This is challenging, as Gemini loves the interplay of opposites, but right now it can feel like being caught in the middle of a 'perfect storm', which is exhausting for the body, emotions and mind. So, where can Gemini find this still point of equilibrium? While the mind can understand the dance of opposites, and even the need to find a place of stillness within that, the mind is not where the answer lies, because the Gemini mind will never remain still for long enough.

The answer lies in turning the attention away from the mind and listening to the heart and the body; it lies in allowing their awareness to 'drop' down into the heart, and trust that the heart knows what is appropriate in every situation. This is not the same as just following the emotions; it is about cultivating an inner equilibrium, which can bring a sense of peace to the heart and thus to the mind. When the inner heart becomes still, it becomes the pivotal point around which everything else can be observed; it is like learning to dance and not losing your balance, or the focused intent required for the tightrope walker to maintain balance.

Somewhere, in between 'this' and 'that', is a still place of emptiness. To find this, Gemini must confront the fear of emptiness, in order to discover the deep inner peace to be found there. This will help connect them with the profound inner stillness emanating from the heart of the Galaxy, around which everything else is constantly revolving.

Tropical Libra = Sidereal Virgo

22 September–23 October

The airy nature of Tropical Libra is underpinned by the Earthy qualities of Sidereal Virgo. The relationship between Air and Earth is not easy to the Air signs; Air and Fire have a more natural affinity with each other, as do Earth and Water. When we look at the larger picture, however, it is the relationship between Earth (the planet) and Air (the atmosphere) that makes Life possible. The movement of air over the surface of the

Earth carries the life-giving moisture of the clouds, which falls as rain to enliven the clods of the Earth; it is an interesting play on words that what makes the difference between the clouds and the clods is 'u' – a good maxim for all Librans to contemplate!

The traditional glyph for Libra is ♎ and it is said to depict the scales or balance; it can equally be seen as a stylized bird, with wings outstretched soaring over the flat plane of the Earth beneath it. At this significant time, Librans are being challenged to really 'get' this relationship between Air and Earth. Tropical Libra wants to soar to the lofty heights and discover the spiritual truths that lie beyond our atmosphere; however, what Libra will find 'out there' is the profoundly earthy energy of the constellation of Virgo, the Divine Mother principle that underpins the Universe.

Librans are being challenged to come down to Earth; they can choose to do this willingly, or with a 'bump'. All of Libra's instincts are to remain up in the lofty heights, particularly as they witness the increasingly unstable changes occurring in our physical, economic and political environment. However, the Air signs are uniquely placed to be able to ascend the higher reaches of the mind to gain an overview of what is occurring 'down below' at the physical and emotional levels. These perceptions are of little value unless Librans can then come back to earth and translate what they see into something meaningful and useful for themselves and others 'on the ground'.

For Librans, this means being in Right Relationship with their bodies and the daily unfolding dramas that they see around them; it means communicating clearly, with sensitivity and using language that can be easily understood by others; it means understanding how to use their spiritual and physical power in ways that are appropriate to whatever their situation.

At this time, Librans' greatest potential for healing themselves lies in developing a healthy attitude of service toward others; this means seeing what is appropriate to each individual situation. Librans have a reputation for wanting to please others – but this can lead to huge energy loss. True service does not mean doing what pleases others, but seeing and responding to what the situation requires. For Libra, this may mean sometimes overriding their idealistic belief systems of what is right, or what 'should be' and taking a more pragmatic, practical, down-to-earth approach to the problems they see around them.

Above all, Librans should remember to include their needs within the bigger picture; failure to do this will result in significant energy loss. The main lesson for Librans is about the appropriate expression of their own self-worth; this means overcoming their common tendency to undervalue themselves, though occasionally some Librans may overvalue their own needs, at the expense of others. This is a fine balancing act, and requires a ruthless emotional honesty about how they feel valued and appreciated.

Librans cannot always expect others to understand what motivates them, as this is often so idealistic as to be completely impractical or meaningless in the real world. But it is important for Librans not to undervalue what they believe, though those beliefs may need some adjustment in the approach to 2012, in order to adapt to the changing needs of the time. The key here lies in flexibility and spontaneity, with the ability to respond quickly and appropriately to the changing needs of each situation. This means living in the moment; when we live in the moment, responses based on cumbersome ideals and belief systems can take too long – what is needed is a spontaneous response, from the heart.

Librans tend to focus on the needs and best interests of others, and often behave in ways that are not always in their own best interests. In the approach to 2012, Librans may find themselves feeling shocked by their extreme responses, but this extremism is there to get them to listen to their own emotional needs. One of the spiritual lessons to be derived from Sidereal Virgo that underpins Tropical Libra is to understand what they need in order to feel spiritually, mentally, emotionally and physically nurtured and nourished. Librans cannot discover this just by wandering around in the refined levels of the upper atmosphere of their minds.

There comes a time when it is necessary to descend to Earth, to find the right kind of sustenance. If Librans get this right, they will become stronger, healthier and able to soar to even more lofty heights in the future. Conversely, if they get too caught up in the concerns of the world, or take in nourishment that is too dense or coarse, then they will lose the ability to fly; it is a question of balance. Librans need enough density, in diet and lifestyle, to remain in connection with the Earth, but not so much density that they feel bound to the Earth and unable to soar upward with their mind.

So for now, Librans need to attend to what is in front of them, come to Earth and deal with day-to-day concerns. They may fully understand that, viewed from another perspective, all of this is merely Illusion, but while we are functioning in a human body, then we are subject to the laws of the Illusion; this is especially true as one set of laws is in the process of falling apart, and the new set has yet to fully manifest. It is important to find the parts that are still stable and reliable, and to understand how to respond to the changing circumstances in the physical environment, so that they do not suddenly find themselves with nowhere to land at all!

The primary purpose for Librans, in the approach to 2012, is to understand how to move beyond the beliefs, opinions and values that were created as a result of their tendency to put others first. In order to create balance around them, it is essential that they always, *always* include themselves and their own needs in any situation. Doing this is not going to turn Librans into selfish, self-seeking egotists; Libra is 'hard-wired' to look out for others, to put the relationship with the 'other' first.

They may have to work especially hard to include themselves in a balanced and equal way; however, not doing this is what causes Librans their greatest problems. Part of Libra's Shadow is generated by the fear of being selfish, and it is this that creates the tendency to overcompensate by focusing too much attention on others. There can also be a fear of confrontation, by standing up for their rights and needs.

Very occasionally, some Librans take this to its opposite extreme, particularly when their belief in an ideal becomes so strong that it takes precedence over any real sensitivity toward the needs of others.

Now, more than ever, is it essential for Librans to get the balance right; to maintain their focus on the needs of others and the world around them, while including themselves in the equation. Not to do this can create a powerful Shadow energy, which can taint and distort Librans' motivation, so that what may appear to be unselfish on the surface actually has a hidden, selfish agenda, motivated at an unconscious level. This is why it is essential for Librans to be as awake and alert to their own needs as they are to the needs of the greater whole, to live fully and consciously in every moment as we approach 2012.

Tropical Aquarius =
Sidereal Capricorn & Aquarius

20 January–19 February

Most of Tropical Aquarius is spanned by the constellation of Capricorn; however, the last 3° or those born between 16 and 19 February, are influenced by the stars of Aquarius itself.

So, once again we have an Air sign being influenced by the more Earthy energies of the constellation in the background. This is an easier combination for Aquarius than it is for the other Air signs, as Aquarius is 'fixed' Air, which brings a more structured quality to Aquarius' way of thinking. The 'fixed' quality contributes to the Aquarian tendency for scientific thinking and a structured, rational approach to life. Aquarius, the Water Bearer, likes to test ideas against known realities in order to see whether they actually 'hold water', and are consistent with what actually occurs or is possible in the 'real world'.

Aquarius is, at the same time, constantly pushing the boundaries of what is known and accepted; this has never been truer than at the present time. We have seen, in previous chapters, how we are all in a time of transition from one Age (Pisces) to the next (Aquarius). As the old Piscean structures are dissolving and collapsing, there is a strong tendency for many Aquarians to overemphasize the 'fixed' quality of the sign, and try to be too rigid or dogmatic about the nature of reality, the nature of politics, the nature of what is right and wrong in their own and others' lives. This distortion of the true energies of Aquarius is currently giving rise to ever-increasing amounts of mindless bureaucracy, creating ever more senseless and detailed laws, rules and restrictions about what we may and may not do.

However, these desperate attempts to control more and more aspects of our daily lives will hopefully be short-lived. They stem from the terrifying (for fixed Aquarius) levels of uncertainty and the awareness that all, yes *all* of the old paradigms are dissolving before our very eyes.

The greatest challenge for Aquarians at this time is how to let go of the structured realities of the past and live in this world of uncertainties, as they unfold at every level of being. There are physical uncertainties to do with the future of our planet, with the security of our financial systems, the integrity of our political systems and the ever more challenging effects of all of this on our physical health and well-being. There are also emotional uncertainties, as the traditional structures of relationships become more diverse and varied, and every person is being challenged to perceive, accept and embrace everyone on the planet as their brother or sister. This is a noble Aquarian ideal, but it can also challenge our levels of emotional tolerance and compassion toward the sufferings and needs of others, particularly when those needs impinge upon long-cherished ideals about personal or national identity. There are mental uncertainties too; as we discover more about the underlying nature of reality, there is the accompanying realization that for all the wonderful things that we do know, there is still an almost infinite amount that we do not know. Every time the sharp end of science reaches an understanding of the underlying atomic structures of the Universe, another level seems to appear behind that.

Is it any wonder that, at the one extreme, Aquarians tries to 'fix' all this uncertainty and create rigid structures and belief systems to say 'this is how it is'? At the other extreme, some Aquarians are eager to relinquish the last 300 years of rational thinking and totally embrace an intuitive approach to the new

Quantum Reality, thereby throwing out the 'new Aquarian baby with the old Piscean bathwater'.

Aquarians are being challenged to let go of their old values, to let go of dogmatic, rational, limited perceptions of what is real or 'scientific', to let go of their security or comfort zones and to let go of their habitual attitudes toward how they have used their imagination and creativity in the past.

At the same time, they are being challenged to find a stable perspective on the world that they see around them, and to find new ways of solving the problems that are arising with increasing speed and diversity. We are all being challenged to truly espouse and live the highest possible Aquarian ideals of brotherhood, sisterhood, loving tolerance and compassion toward all beings on the planet.

Aquarians are also being challenged to accommodate other levels and dimensions of reality into their thinking if they are to gain a true picture of reality as it is. The fear-based backlash is to become totally fixed on the physical Universe as the only reality – if you can't measure it, then it doesn't exist!

Finally, Aquarians are being challenged to understand how to express their personal individual will, while accommodating the collective will, taking into account all of the above factors. It is a tall order for Aquarians and for all of us, but it is one that we must all rise to.

Uranus, the ruler of Aquarius, holds the key to how to negotiate all of these dynamic and unpredictable changes – by living, fully present in each moment, we can realize that we have all of the internal and external resources that we need, to respond to the changing demands of the time. We can only live in the moment when we learn to let go of restrictive, dogmatic or fixed ideas about the nature of the world around us, or about our own limitations or ability to respond appropriately.

CHAPTER 11

HOW 2012 AFFECTS WATER SIGNS: CANCER, SCORPIO, PISCES

Water is concerned with the feelings, emotions and the consciousness of the soul. Water is the life-giving element that sustains and nourishes our inner life. If our feelings are unable to flow freely, then the soul remains arid and dry. Being in touch with our inner feeling world enables us to fully experience Life, and interact meaningfully with others.

Through the highs and lows of our emotional experiences, the soul becomes transformed, purified, uplifted and expanded, until it is capable of experiencing the bliss of Unconditional Love. This may overwhelm the personality, if there is insufficient emotional experience and maturity to integrate it.

Water is self-purifying and self-healing. The keys to understanding this element are the ability to develop trust and the courage to follow our deepest convictions. It is at its best when able to flow freely, yielding and in doing so, overcoming obstacles in its path. Sometimes it is a trickle, sometimes a torrent, yet always it retains its true nature. Water is about purity, clarity, healing, nourishment, and the expression of love, compassion and empathy; all of which helps to create abundance and fullness of life.

Tropical Cancer = Sidereal Gemini

21 June–22 July

As we move to the Water signs, we find that they are underpinned by constellations associated with the Air element. This means we are living in an age when the emotions are tempered by the clarity and objectivity of the mind. The emotionally nurturing, caring, self-protective and family-oriented qualities of Tropical Cancer are being influenced by the more objective, rational and social qualities of Sidereal Gemini. This has the effect of extending Cancer's sense of family, clan or tribe outward; Cancerians' natural tendency to look out for and protect their own is constantly expanding, challenging them to accommodate an increasingly broad diversity in those whom they accept as part of their wider 'family'.

This is the key to understanding the challenges faced by Cancerians in the approach to 2012. Cancerians are hard-wired to make immediate family, clan, tribe or nation their main priority. Now they are awakening to the reality that the whole of Humanity is their family, and that they cannot afford to show favouritism, or merely protect their own interests, if that conflicts with the wider interest. Sidereal Gemini challenges Tropical Cancer to understand that Right Relationship must extend toward everyone on the planet, not in some vague, generalized, conceptual way, but in a way that acknowledges the feelings and emotional needs of everyone as unique individuals. The more that Cancerians do this, the more empowered they will feel, because they will know in their hearts that everyone is their brother, sister, mother or father.

This is a challenge; Cancerians like to know where they stand, where they belong, who is family and who is not. Now, it is imperative to dissolve these ancient values about boundaries and separation between tribes and nations; to dissolve divisive attitudes toward those with different beliefs, religions or customs; to wake up to the uniqueness of every individual, including themselves.

Cancerians are being reminded of our ancient common origin with all human beings; when this is experienced as a felt sense, it will influence the ways in which they use their creativity in service to others. When we truly *know* in our hearts that everyone is our brother or sister, it has a profound influence on the ways we behave toward them in every arena of life.

For Cancerians, it is particularly relevant to dissolve any divisive feelings toward those who appear to be 'other' than themselves; when they understand that such feelings stem from their own unresolved Shadow qualities, they will come to discover what they fear within their own nature. Behind this is an innate awareness that divisive feelings have a profoundly disturbing effect on the planet herself.

It is one thing to have a conceptual understanding that the Earth is a single organism, and that we humans are a part of that organism. The full implication of this is that if one part of this organism feels alienated or antagonistic toward any other part, then it becomes like a body divided against itself.

This is like someone believing that their hand is disconnected from their foot, and failing to recognize that each has their own function and must cooperate in order to work together as one. Such a belief of disconnection will eventually create a physical problem of coordination between the hand

and the foot. If we extend these beliefs so that whole nations or sectors of society feel such separation, this then resonates into the energetic structure of the Earth, and creates blocks and disharmonies in the very fabric of the land where people live.

Cancerians are being called to understand these connections between strongly held attitudes, and their effects on both people, and the Earth herself. The Earth is our Mother; when we abuse or disrespect her or when we are constantly arguing or warring amongst ourselves, we cause her stress just as surely as if we behaved this way in our own family. Eventually, she may respond to that stress by admonishing and disciplining us, in order to wake us up to what we are doing. Alternatively, she may become stuck, or blocked, or may cave in to the pressure; when this happens, and the free flow of energy in the Earth becomes blocked, then this has a knock-on effect on human behaviour, and a downward spiral develops.

Cancerians are being called to understand the relationships and interactions between our emotional attitudes, the physical structures of our societies and nations, and the Earth. Some will understand this in a small way, others in a big way. What matters is that Cancerians recognize their responsibility in this and use all of their creative instincts to ensure that such disharmonies do not arise, first within their own feelings, then within their family, then within their village, town or city, then within their region and country. The Water signs know that any 'ripples' they create in their immediate environment will have an effect, no matter how subtle or small, on the whole of their emotional and physical environment.

Cancerians are uniquely placed to understand how to wake up to their responsibility to communicate these truths to others; it is as if Cancer's natural feeling sensitivity is 'on alert' to the implications of their feeling responses to whatever is going on around them. This is jolting Cancerians out of their emotional comfort zones, making them acutely aware of their responsibility to take the lead in helping others to see how our emotional responses shape the world around us.

When we change our habitual emotional responses, then the world changes too. This is the crux of Cancer's service to the world in these times. Firstly they need to change their own emotional response patterns; this requires them to be awake and alert in each moment, observing that when they do that, then the world responds to that change. Secondly, they need to lovingly communicate this with others and enable them to understand how to do this in their own lives. All the while, Cancer is challenged not to simply fall back into old, habitual emotional attitudes. By living fully from the heart in each moment, Cancerians have the opportunity to completely restructure their beliefs; by doing this, they will restructure their world, and the resulting ripples will be felt by all around them. That is their greatest gift to the world, at this time.

Tropical Scorpio = Sidereal Virgo & Libra

23 October–21 November

The first third of watery Tropical Scorpio is underpinned by the constellation of earthy Virgo; the last two-thirds is influenced by the constellation of airy Libra. Those born 23–31 October will feel Virgo's influence, enabling Scorpio's depth and intensity to feel a sense of self-containment. Those born between 1 and 21 November will be dependent on the airy influences of Libra, so will be more likely to fluctuate between calms and storms. This will depend on prevailing circumstances and relationships – at times the waters of Scorpio may remain serene and calm, while at others they may be whipped up into a storm.

At the 2012 Solstice, Saturn holds a pivotal position. It is in the Tropical Zodiac sign of Scorpio, and poised midway between the Sidereal Zodiac constellations of Virgo and Libra. In this position, Saturn draws down both the practical discernment of Virgo and the mental equilibrium of Libra, in order to hold and maintain the balance of Scorpio's deepest emotions.

Of all the zodiac signs, Scorpio is the most willing to explore and accept the darker aspects of the human psyche. Since Saturn represents the personal Shadow in every astrology chart, it could not be better placed for the deep shift that will occur in 2012. Scorpios have the potential to understand how to deal with this shadow energy and help Saturn create a healthy balance between the deepest emotions, mind and body.

Saturn, in this position, dares Scorpio to confront its darkest emotional and existential fears; Saturn also demands that we confront our individual and collective grief over the long-term loss of a meaningful spiritual connection with the Earth and the Cosmos. When we fully allow ourselves to feel that deep sense of loss, created by centuries of disconnection from the natural rhythms and cycles of our planet, this can feel overwhelming. It is as if we have been collectively staving off this moment, ever since we first began to become 'civilized' and move away from our dependence on natural cycles. The presence of Virgo and Libra behind Tropical Scorpio, however, can help to bring a sense of perspective and a level of mental detachment, so that we can move through our grief, rather than becoming overwhelmed by it.

Scorpio occurs at that time of year, in the Northern Hemisphere, when everything is beginning to die off and fall back into the Earth; this is a perfectly natural and necessary part of the cycle. Yet when it happens, as now, in the world of commerce and global finance, it is perceived as something wrong or tragic, and we look for where to lay the blame. If we really want to apportion blame, then it must lie with those who insist on perpetual and continuous growth. This is not natural, and in order to support the illusion of limitless growth, we have created another unnatural phenomenon – debt.

Scorpio is telling us that we all (not just Scorpios) need to take a long hard look at the reality of just how far we, as a species, have strayed from our connection with natural rhythms and cycles. The effect of the midwinter Sun emerging from the darkness of the Cosmic Womb of Creation means that we each have a unique opportunity to be spiritually reborn from this 'Cosmic Winter' that has lasted for 13,000 years. The magnification effect of the Galactic Solstice is so powerful that we cannot escape the consequences of this loss of connection with the Natural Order, unless we are willing to confront our deepest, most primal feelings about that loss.

Scorpios know that if they are not prepared to look at their own darkness, then it eats away at the soul, creating chaos and disorder. They also know that when they dare to look into the darkness, there lies a wealth of creative possibilities, locked within the stuck and unexpressed emotions that have been festering away in the Unconscious. The key to our healing is to feel the grief; yet everything in the outside world of commerce, materialism and the busy-ness of life conspires to make us 'comfortably numb' and to distract us from ever getting close to feeling the deep grief within the collective human soul.

Grief can be the most profound and transformative of the emotions, because it holds the key to understanding and eventually transcending the impermanence of life. When we accept grief, we accept that all things must die, or be transformed.

For Scorpios, 2012 offers profound healing potential. When we are stuck in unexpressed grief, we are disempowered; if we believe that death is a finality, as opposed to part of a cycle, then that can feel hopeless and disempowering. As we watch the daily extinction of hundreds of species on the planet, or the damage caused by oil spills in the oceans, or the threat of nuclear disaster, or the unpredictability of increasing numbers of natural disasters, it is hard not to feel at the mercy of forces that seem beyond our control. The sense of disempowerment becomes exaggerated when we simply run around trying to 'fix it', by supporting measures 'so that it can't happen again', or by putting pressure on the perpetrators of corruption or incompetence, only to discover that a few months later they are back to their old tricks again.

Healing begins when we stop and allow ourselves to feel the sadness, the fear and the grief, because hidden deep within those feelings is the true gold within our being.

For Scorpios, that gold lies in the knowledge that everything proceeds in cycles; the deeper our willingness to let go of the past, the more powerful the possibilities for transformation and positive change in the future. Above all else, Scorpios need to be true to their deepest emotional values at this crucial time; the worst thing is for them to become caught up in the existential fears or expectations of others. It is essential that they follow the creative urges that spring from their inner sense of knowing what is right for them, and from where they need to draw their nourishment. It is crucial that they are not dependent on others for answering their physical or emotional needs. Again, this can be the hardest thing for Scorpios to do, as they thrive on deep, intense connections, interactions and emotional exchange.

So how do Scorpios sustain their need for intense involvement, while not becoming dependent on others?

This will be different for each individual, according to their personality and natural tendencies; the key is for them to listen to their inner voice and ask themselves what are the unique creative qualities that they can apply in service for the good of society and for the benefit of the planet. Then it is important to remain true to their core values, and act in ways that express these. For Scorpios, the key to being in Right Relationship with others will depend upon the level of honesty with which they communicate what they feel and see. This honesty may be shocking or disturbing to others, but it is needed in order to keep themselves alert and wake others up to what is going on around them. The point here is not to shock for its own sake, but to make others more aware.

It is important that Scorpios acknowledge that they can be in touch with their feelings at a much deeper level than many others; so part of their responsibility is first to acknowledge those feelings, and then communicate them with others, in ways that will bring insight. It is important to approach this in constructive ways that are respectful of the emotional values of others. This is not about forcing others to understand how Scorpio is feeling; it is more about sharing the feeling insights that can be of mutual benefit.

The more Scorpios are able to communicate with others clearly, honestly and respectfully, the more empowered they will feel. If that communication is coming from a place of personal hurt or feeling 'wronged', however, then it is important for Scorpio to own their feelings and not to project them onto others. This is the key to Scorpio dealing creatively with any feelings that come from the Shadow, and understanding the need to temper those feelings with the discernment of Virgo and the detachment of Libra.

Tropical Pisces = Sidereal Aquarius & Pisces

19 February–21 March

The first two-thirds of watery Tropical Pisces is underpinned with the airy energy of Sidereal Aquarius and the last third with the watery energy of Sidereal Pisces. This means that those Pisceans born between 19 February and 12 March are working to integrate the more structured, ordered mind energies of Sidereal Aquarius into their highly fluid and changeable emotional nature. Those born between 13 and 21 March are more aligned with the pure watery energy of Sidereal Pisces, which can either amplify their changeable emotional nature, or can bring into play sublime qualities of spiritual inspiration, devotion and the ability to feel profound levels of compassion and spiritual bliss.

For Pisceans, 2012 is concerned with self-healing; this means discovering how to feel comfortable about merging their consciousness with the greater whole, without completely losing their sense of individual identity. This begins with Pisceans realizing that their essential self is not just the product of their environment or upbringing, nor does it result from the belief systems that they have developed in response to, or as a reaction to, their early environment or family dynamic. Pisces is so immersed in the world of the feelings that it can be difficult to separate their individual spiritual essence out from the external influences and emotional response patterns that have been laid down from an early age.

There is a huge paradox at play here; in order for Pisceans to heal themselves, by understanding and embracing their relationship to the whole of humanity, they first need to develop a strong sense of individuality. This can mean standing alone in their beliefs, which can be daunting because Pisceans are so sensitive to the feeling-world around them that it is often easier to go with the flow of the prevailing collective feeling in which they are immersed.

The deep healing offered to Pisceans by the changing energies of 2012, however, means finding how to stand in Right Relationship with the world and the Universe around them. It is like a small fish learning how to swim with the vast, changing currents of the times, without becoming overwhelmed, taken off course, or completely losing their individual identity to the 'shoal instinct'.

Like everyone else, Pisceans are being challenged to discover how to be in Right Relationship with others. For Pisces this means seeing into the individual needs of each soul around them; it is a fine balancing act for Pisceans to honour their own inner sensitivities, while expressing their feelings and ideas in ways that will be spiritually uplifting for others. In particular, Pisceans are being called to understand and respond to the group dynamics that are at play in whatever circumstances they find themselves.

In order to do this, they need to develop a fine sense of their boundaries. This can be the most difficult thing for Pisceans to master, and they cannot apply a 'one-size-fits-all' approach to how they define their boundaries. These will change, often quite radically, according to who they are with, and their environment. The key to knowing if they are getting this right is whether they are creating circumstances that bring them emotional, mental and spiritual nourishment, bearing in mind that what has worked for them in the past may not work now.

Pisces has to be able to live and respond to changing circumstances, in the moment. There are no rules about how to do this, except that whatever the response, it needs to come from the heart. At the same time, the mind needs to become aware of whether that heart response is genuinely spontaneous, or simply repeating a past reaction pattern.

This is important, whether they are responding to others, or to a part of themselves. In relating to others, Pisceans need to listen to the inner voice, and balance what that is telling them against the needs, opinions and beliefs of others. This may require a surrender of what their personal will desires, in favour of the will of the greater whole, but not at the expense of too much personal compromise; so, it is crucial for Pisces to ask 'what is the right response here?', and then to wait for the answer to come to them. When dealing with the self, this may mean going against long-held values, and adjusting emotional responses accordingly. This is not about self-compromise but rather about finding the deeper principles that lie behind convictions; it may also mean recognizing when they have been living according to 'values' that may be the result of stuck emotional reaction patterns from the past.

Pisceans need to be recreating their values in every moment, rather than having any fixed sense of values. It is important to understand that whatever their response to different situations, they are quite literally 'weaving' and creating the fabric of their lives by their emotional responses to the world around them. The mind can observe this and see that 'if I respond in this way, then this will happen, but if I respond in that way, then that will happen'.

This is all about understanding that their emotional responses create their world. This is true for everyone, but at this time, Pisceans are getting an object lesson in this, with some very rapid responses occurring, so they can quickly see the results of their thoughts and feelings. Pisceans are learning that the fabric of the Universe is not fixed; the fluidity and changeability of their lives, which can be so frustrating and confusing at times, is affected by their own emotional responses. What brings the greatest healing to Pisceans is the realization that they hold the keys to creating their own world, by how they react to the vast currents of energy in which we are all immersed. When Pisceans understand that they are, at one and the same time, both separate from and at One with these currents of energy, then they will understand how to negotiate and flow with them effortlessly.

Chapter 12
BEYOND 2012 (2013–16)

This chapter gives a brief overview of the most significant alignments occurring from January 2013 to December 2016. The December Solstice in 2016 will mark the final emergence of the solstice Sun from the 'birth canal' of the 'Dark Rift' of the Galactic Equator. By then, the 'new consciousness' will be firmly rooted into the collective human psyche, and will be increasingly manifesting out in the world.

It is useful to reiterate here that everything proceeds in stages. Each new stage brings a consciousness shift, which prepares us for the next one. From our present perspective, it can be difficult, if not impossible, for us to comprehend just how things will be several years into the future. Only by experiencing each stage of change can our consciousness grasp what comes next. This is like the difference between reading a map to plan your journey, and actually undertaking the journey; it is not possible, from just reading the map, to anticipate the rich variety of experiences, unexpected meetings and turns of events that may occur once we actually embark on our journey.

What follows is based on the 'maps' of the astrological patterns emerging after 2012. As 2012 represents such a powerful

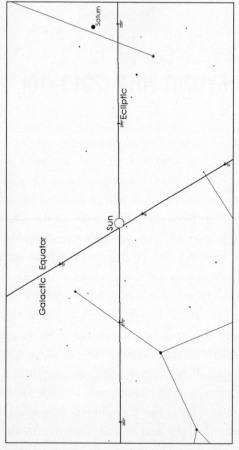

The Sun leaves the Galactic Equator on 21 December 2016

Image produced by Chris Marriott's SkyMap Pro

pivotal point in the orientation of our collective consciousness, everything should appear very different to us after that.

2013

The first major alignment of 2013 is when Juno becomes exactly conjunct with Pluto on 14 January; they are then joined by Venus on 17 January. Venus brings the understanding of what Right Relationship means at the personality level, and in the context of our everyday relationships. It shows how we can live the spiritual ideals that have been emerging ever since Juno aligned with the Galactic Centre, back in 2008.

On 12 February, Mårs becomes exactly conjunct with Chiron, removing and healing any emotional restraints that have been preventing us from moving forward. On 20 February, the Sun conjuncts Neptune, which is joined by Venus on 28 February, at the same time as the Sun moves on to conjunct Chiron. This is like a domino effect, with everything falling into place in rapid sequence. This will provide the energy to manifest the visions that we have been holding, so that now we can begin to live according to our heart's true dream.

However, from 18 February, we will once again be dealing with a retrograde Saturn, putting the brakes on until 8 July, while we confront any lingering inner resistances, and complete unfinished business. We will receive help for this by a sequence of very favourable Grand Trines and Kite patterns.

Many Grand Trines and Kites

Grand Trines occur whenever three planets form a perfect equilateral triangle pattern in the heavens (each 120° apart);

this creates a positive, harmonious flow between the qualities of the planets involved, making available an abundance of creative energy.

The planets' positions around the zodiac, during a Grand Trine (GT), usually mean they are all within zodiac signs of the same element; this congruity of elements enhances the harmonious quality of the GT, emphasizing spiritual/intuitive qualities for Fire GTs, physical/practical qualities for Earth GTs, mental/intellectual qualities for Air GTs and emotional/empathic qualities for Water GTs.

When another planet moves into a position midway (60°) between two of the GT planets, this creates a 'Kite' pattern; a Kite is like a Grand Trine and a half, enabling even more creative potentials to manifest.

From mid-April to mid-September 2013, several Grand Trines occur, principally involving Saturn, Ceres, Chiron and Neptune. This is a golden time for healing our relationship with the Earth, for letting go of old destructive attitudes and emotional attachment to ways that have been damaging the Earth, and our relationship with Her.

On 17 September, the Moon's North Node conjuncts Saturn and Venus, all in Scorpio. This will bring the final crystallization of new and enduring attitudes toward all of our relationships, enhancing our ability to live the ideals of Right Relations, brought by Juno.

The remainder of 2013 will be concerned with applying these new levels of awareness to the challenges of constantly living from a place of Right Relations. We will be truly learning how to live out the Aquarian ideals of universal brotherhood and sisterhood; how to balance our needs as individuals with the needs of the larger group, and how to marry the intuitive intelligence of the heart with the rational intelligence of the mind.

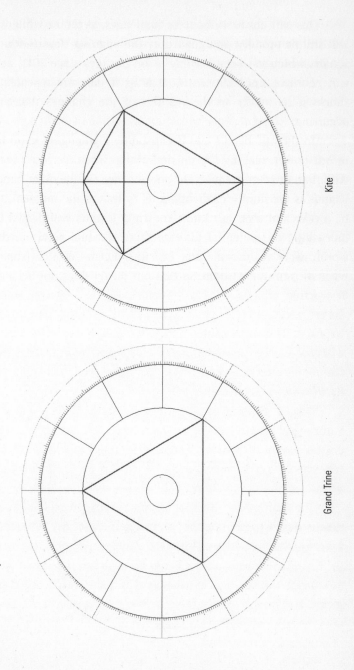

Kite

Grand Trine

This will not be without its challenges, as all the while we will still be prodded and goaded by the ongoing Uranus–Pluto square, which has been keeping us on our toes since 2011, and will continue until May 2015. It is as if they are repeatedly shocking us awake to the realities of the changes that are occurring.

On the one hand Pluto is constantly challenging us to be in our power, making life uncomfortable when we lose touch with that, or when we give our power away. On the other hand, Uranus is constantly challenging us to live in the moment, to be awake and trust our inner knowing. Uranus will persist in unleashing our potential for expressing spiritual power in the world, while at the same time insisting that we do that from a place of intuitive wisdom, so that our power does not become destructive.

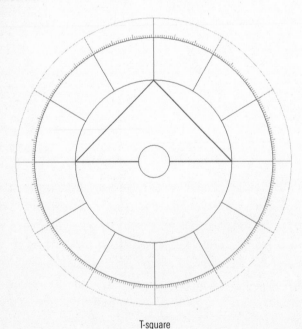

T-square

On 22 December 2013, Jupiter joins this dynamic, moving into opposition with Pluto, thereby completing a 'T-square' pattern, at the apex of the triangle with Uranus and Pluto; this pattern will persist until the end of May 2014.

2014

These three 'heavyweights' will be pulling in different directions simultaneously. Jupiter in Cancer will be encouraging us to bring to fruition our most optimistic vision for a more compassionate and caring world. Opposing this, Pluto in Capricorn, the voice of pragmatism, will insist on the need to maintain the balance of power in our personal lives, and in the larger political arena. Poised midway between these two, Uranus in Aries will make instantaneous intuitive decisions and judgments about whether to be swayed more toward Jupiter's optimism or Pluto's pragmatism.

Uranus is the ruling planet for the Age of Aquarius and it may seem like we are being stretched to the limit in order to get us to think, feel and act from a 'Uranian' perspective. This will continually take us beyond reason, and beyond what is known, in order to stimulate our intuitive knowing of what is right for us.

Jupiter will extend the possibilities of what we can imagine or vision, until we reach that 'aha' moment of realization about how to approach problems in new and more enlightened ways. Meanwhile, Pluto creates a sense of urgency for us to reach that point of realization, because maintaining the status quo will disempower us and damage our environment and us. Each time we reach such a point of realization it will bring a sense of relief, enabling movement and change, before the tension builds up again and takes us toward the next level of realization and release.

A Grand Cross

By mid-April 2014, retrograde Mars will have joined this pattern, opposing Uranus and thereby creating a powerful Grand Cross.

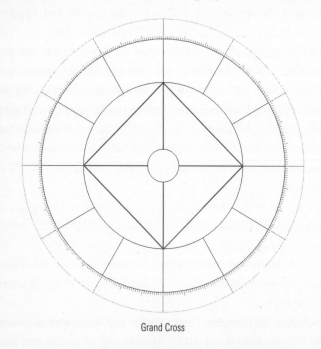

Grand Cross

In mid-May, Mars is joined by retrogrades Vesta, Ceres and the Moon's North Node, in a stellium that brings the Grand Cross to a powerful climax, before it starts to break up at the end of May.

The combination of retrogrades Mars, Vesta, Ceres and the North Node brings a tense and powerful message, to resist falling back into old ways of expressing our will, by overriding the sensitivity of the heart and causing damage to ourselves and to the Earth. Uranus, now joined by Mercury, holds the key to using our intuitive intelligence to make huge leaps of awareness and faith, in order to come up with new and unexpected solutions to our problems. Now the Mercury mind will begin to understand how the application of this new 'Uranian' intelligence really works, and how we can consciously call it up when we need it, rather than having to wait until we are stretched to our uttermost limits before it kicks in.

By the time that Mars, Ceres and Vesta have all gone direct and become exactly conjunct with the Moon's Node from 12 to 15 July, this will have brought our will and heart into complete alignment with one another, forging a 'new' spiritual faculty of knowing and expressing our spiritual purpose, in complete alignment with our sense of responsibility toward the Earth.

Many Grand Trines and Kites

Grand Trines and Kites occur fairly infrequently. Unfolding throughout the remainder of 2014, and most of 2015, however, is a rare sequence of Grand Trines, one after the other, with several Kites interspersed. These herald a time of great positivity, abundance, harmony, creativity and the resolution of inner and outer conflicts.

In the days leading up to the exact stellium of Mars, Ceres, Vesta and the Moon's North Node, a powerful Grand Trine in Water signs forms. This lasts from 3 to 16 July, between the Sun (in Cancer), Saturn (in Scorpio) and Chiron (in Pisces). This Grand Trine brings a deep healing of humanity's emotional

Shadow, enabling the clearing of ancient resistances and blocks in our ability to feel and express Unconditional Love toward all of our fellow beings.

Within a few days of it dissolving, the Grand Trine returns on 22 July, but with Mercury in place of the Sun. Then Mercury moves on and is replaced by Venus from 29 July until 7 August. Mercury's and Venus' involvement means that the healing taking place at deep unconscious levels of the emotional body can be understood by the mind, integrated at the conscious emotional level, then carried through into our relationships.

On 12 August, another powerful Grand Trine forms, again in Water signs, between Neptune (in Pisces), Juno (in Cancer) and Ceres, Vesta and Mars (all together in Scorpio). This lasts until 19 September, enabling us to know in our hearts how to act with clear intent, and apply the energy of Unconditional Love in all of our relationships, but most importantly in our relationship with the Earth.

Yet another Grand Trine forms on 29 September, this time in Fire signs, between Uranus conjunct Moon's South Node (in Aries), Jupiter (in Leo) and Mars (in Sagittarius). As Uranus continues the process of letting go of the past, this frees us up to express the full extent of our creative powers and abilities. Within a week, the Grand Trine transforms into a 'Kite', bringing the Moon's North Node, Sun and Venus to the head of the Kite; this will enable us to express our creativity in ways that are fully aligned with our spiritual purpose. This pattern lasts until 13 October.

On 29 October, another Grand Trine forms, with Uranus (in Aries), Juno (in Leo) and Vesta (in Sagittarius). Whereas the previous GT was enabling the expression of the male aspect of our creativity through Jupiter and Mars, this one enables the expression of the feminine aspect and balances the male expression, by ensuring that we remain in Right Relationship with our hearts, so we can radiate that out to everyone around us.

On 16 November, Ceres moves into Vesta's position, and is joined by Venus on 23 November; this will enable us to feel and express real love for Mother Earth. Then on 28 November, the Moon's Node takes up position at the apex of another Kite, reinforcing that our main purpose now is to love the Earth.

Ceres and Venus are joined by the Sun on 2 December, then by Mercury three days later, bringing about an integration of heart and mind in the ways that we express our love for the Earth. This Kite pattern persists until 11 December. Juno turns retrograde on 16 December, which will bring to the surface any still unresolved relationship patterns.

More Grand Trines – 2015

On 16 January, this Grand Trine re-forms, now between Uranus (in Aries), Juno (in Leo) and now Pallas Athene (in Sagittarius). Pallas brings her quality of insight and detachment, enabling us to perceive with clarity any old, negative patterns of relationship that still need to be released. This GT transforms into a Kite on 26 January, with retrograde Mercury at its head, creating the urge to carry things forward; but we will probably be unable to see exactly how to do this until Mercury turns direct on 13 February. The Grand Trine dissolves on 18 February.

The very next day, *another* Grand Trine forms between Juno (still retrograde in Leo), Saturn (in Sagittarius) and Mars and Venus (just in the last two degrees of Pisces). The presence of Mars and Venus, just hanging on at the end of Pisces, means that this pattern is concerned with making wise choices in our relationships, so that we can finally and fully let go of any remnants of the old emotional patterns from the Piscean Age.

Venus Conjunct Mars – Balancing Feminine and Masculine

On 22 February, Venus and Mars become exactly conjunct in the first degree of Aries, signifying the potential to move freely forward and begin a new cycle of the balanced expression of masculine and feminine in all of our relationships. This male–female balance triggers the energetic quality that will underpin this 5,125-year cycle of the fifth Sun. The Grand Trine persists until 5 March, when Venus and Mars will have moved into position either side of Uranus, allowing the release of these new frequencies of female–male balance into collective consciousness.

On 20 March, another Grand Trine re-forms, between Juno (now direct in Leo), Saturn (in Sagittarius) and the Sun (in Aries). Mercury joins this pattern on 31 March, as the Sun conjuncts the Moon's South Node, which continues to hold this position until the GT dissolves on 15 April. The presence of the Sun, then Mercury aligning with the South Node, means that our minds will be able to fully understand what is being released, and why it needs to be released. Then we can collectively draw upon the rich experiences of our recent past, to consolidate new ways of expressing and maintaining Right Relationships in the future.

On 4 May, still another Grand Trine appears, this time with the Moon's North Node (in Libra), Ceres (in Aquarius), and Mercury (in Gemini). This is the first of the Grand Trines to be in Air signs, signifying that what has been felt by the Water signs and intuited by the Fire signs can now become conscious at the level of the mind. This GT transforms into a Kite on 8 May, as Juno approaches conjunction with Jupiter, at the apex of the Kite.

Juno Conjuncts Jupiter – The Divine Marriage

The conjunction of Juno and Jupiter represents the inner (divine) marriage of the feminine and masculine. Juno and Jupiter are queen and king of the gods, so their union represents a profound moment in the unfolding of this new cycle of the fifth Sun, and the deepening of the balanced expression of the feminine and the masculine within collective consciousness. The alignments of Venus and Mars created balance at the personality level; the alignment of Juno and Jupiter will create balance at the soul level.

The Kite dissolves on 12 May then, as Juno reaches exact conjunction with Jupiter on 17 May, the GT in Air re-forms with the Moon's North Node (in Libra), Ceres (in Aquarius) and Mars (in Gemini). As the divine feminine and divine masculine become as one in our hearts, Mars the spiritual warrior finally understands how to act in ways that honour and fulfil the destiny of the Earth. Then Mars and the Sun stand firm in opposition to retrograde Saturn, challenging any perpetuation of old patriarchal patterns of confrontation, duality and destructive competition.

With the GT still present in Air, a second Grand Trine forms in Fire signs, on 30 May. This is between Uranus (in Aries), Jupiter with Juno (in Leo) and Pallas Athene (retrograde in Sagittarius); Pallas brings the anticipation of a complete release of the past, and the influx of healing energies that can be fully awakened by the marriage of the feminine and masculine within us.

In addition to the above two Grand Trines, a third Grand Trine forms two days later in Water signs; Venus (in Cancer) trines Saturn (just in Sagittarius) and Vesta (in Pisces). Venus brings the energy of love to heal the emotional body, by dissolving any lingering resistances in the heart.

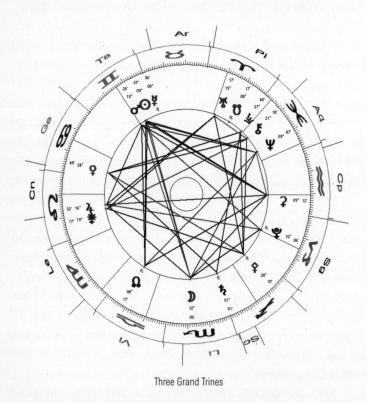

Three Grand Trines

On 5 June, Mars in conjunction with the Sun takes up position at the apex of a Kite pattern (above the Fire GT). By 9 June, Venus (now in Leo) has also moved into position at the apex of a different Kite pattern (above the Air GT). So now Venus and Mars are each at the head of their own Kite. This indicates the firm establishment within the collective consciousness of a

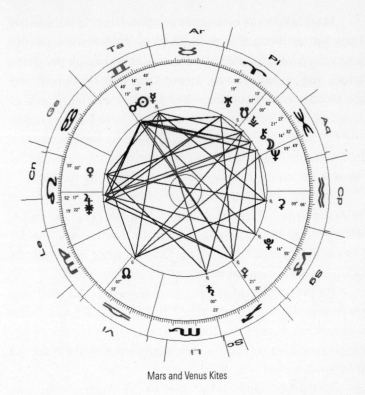

Mars and Venus Kites

balanced expression of the masculine and the feminine, in such a way that each maintains its integrity, identity and creativity as equals, while at the same time maintaining Right Relationship with each another.

This amazing sequence of Mars conjunct Venus, followed by Juno conjunct Jupiter, followed by the two Kites, with Mars and Venus at their heads, means that the energy of balanced relationship will become more and more freely available, as we progress further into the cycle of the fifth Sun. This is just the very beginning of a new era of balanced relationship.

Mars and Venus both move on, dissolving their respective Kites on 17 June, but continuing to release their creative potentials into the collective consciousness through the Grand Trines that remain. The Air Grand Trine (left by Venus), with the Moon's North Node, Ceres and Mercury, continues until 27 June; the Fire Grand Trine (left by Mars), with Uranus, Jupiter and Pallas, continues until 3 July. This allows time for the new feminine archetypes to become integrated by the mind and for the new masculine archetypes to be integrated by the spirit.

And yet another Grand Trine forms on 27 July between Vesta (in Aries), Mercury conjunct Sun (in Leo) and Pallas, which is also briefly conjunct Moon (in Sagittarius). This GT lasts until 12 August, uniting the inner spiritual heart with the heart-mind, the rational mind and the intuitive mind.

On 20 August, Mars (in Leo) takes over from what was previously the Sun's position and re-forms the GT with Pallas (in Sagittarius) and Vesta (in Aries). This will bring the energy of the masculine will into perfect alignment with the heart and the intuitive mind.

Retrograde Venus joins Mars on 22 August, then goes direct on 7 September, and takes over from Mars' position in the GT on 14 September. So again, we will see the continuing harmonious dance between Mars and Venus, as the male and female energies of the fifth Sun move ever deeper into alignment and balance.

Meanwhile retrograde Uranus joins retrograde Vesta in the Grand Trine on 4 September. On 8 September, Mercury moves into position to transform the GT into a Kite. Mercury (in Libra) will bring to conscious awareness the creative possibilities of this new-found balance between the masculine and feminine, and between heart and mind. This Kite dissolves on 23 September, while the GT continues until 2 October.

The Energy Changes

After nearly 15 months of harmonious and creative Grand Trines and Kites, from 20 September the energy begins to intensify, as several oppositions begin to form. Vesta and the Moon's South Node oppose Juno, Moon's North Node and the Sun; Mercury opposes Uranus; Neptune opposes Mars and Jupiter.

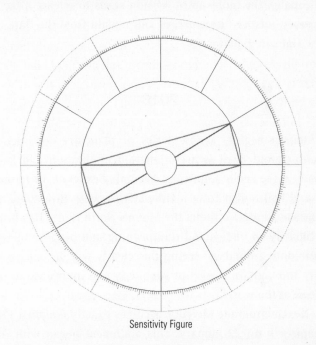

Sensitivity Figure

These gradually build in intensity until the 21 December Solstice, creating several 'Sensitivity' figures. 'Sensitivity' figures create intense patterns, producing tension build-up and reaction. Their purpose is to push us to view the issues concerned from new and more fully conscious levels of perception.

Uranus, Vesta, Chiron and Neptune are all retrograde on one side of the chart, respectively in opposition to Mercury,

Juno and Sun, Mars and Jupiter, all of which are moving direct. The retrogrades are 'testing' our personal planets to see how well we have integrated the new energies of the masculine and feminine; these can be easy enough to maintain when everything is flowing and harmonious, but not so easy when things begin to get tense and confrontational. This will be a testing time.

Finally, the build-up of tension starts to release after the December Solstice Sun emerges, once again from the Dark Rift of the Galactic Equator.

2016

As January begins, a new series of planetary conjunctions start to unfold. First is a conjunction of the Sun and Pallas Athene, at the end of Capricorn, becoming exact on 19 January. Sun and Pallas also form a Grand Trine, with the Moon, and retrograde Jupiter conjunct the Moon's North Node. This brings the capacity to understand the meaning and purpose of what is unfolding around us; seeing this clearly will depend on our ability to maintain a level of simplicity and innocence in how we look at the world.

Next, retrograde Mercury becomes exactly conjunct Pluto in Capricorn on 22 January. This alignment began with their first contact on 19 December 2015, and will bring into sharp focus the need to develop physical and mental stamina, so we can keep pace with the speed of the changes.

On 23 January, retrograde Jupiter becomes exactly conjunct the Moon's North Node in Virgo, in opposition to Chiron, conjunct Moon's South Node. This pattern indicates the need to stay focused on our spiritual purpose, remembering all that has been healing over previous years. It is important not become impatient, or get carried away with overextending ourselves or going beyond our present capabilities.

On 4 February, Vesta becomes exactly conjunct Uranus in Aries, awakening and aligning the inner heart with the changing rhythms and cycles of the new energies. Vesta and Uranus are at the head of a whole string of planets, stretching out behind them from Aries to Scorpio – everything is following their lead.

Vesta conjunct Uranus

As Vesta starts to pull away, ahead of Uranus, the inner spiritual heart takes the lead. She carries in her train the insight of Uranus, the healing of Chiron, the surrender of Neptune, the nurture of Ceres, the power of the Sun, the clarity and intelligence of Pallas and Mercury, the spiritual power of Pluto, the love of Venus, the stability of Saturn, all driven from behind by the powerful will of Mars in Right Relationship with Juno. Meanwhile, Jupiter remains in close conjunction with the Moon's North Node in Virgo, keeping the mind patiently and resolutely focused on the larger purpose.

By 5 April Vesta, now in Taurus, forms a Grand Trine with retrograde Jupiter (in Virgo) and Pluto (in Capricorn) – finally, there is a Grand Trine in Earth, uniting the spiritual heart and spiritual will, and bringing our soul's vision and purpose into full manifestation.

On 16 April, Mercury joins this pattern as it conjuncts Vesta, enabling the mind to grasp what this means in practice. The GT gradually builds, as the Sun and Venus move up to join Mercury (now retrograde), while Vesta goes on ahead. The combination of Mercury, Sun and Venus will enable the heart and mind to know just how to manifest our vision and purpose. The GT continues until 7 June, with Mercury, the last to leave, ensuring that we know what to do next.

Meanwhile Sun, Venus and Vesta move on into opposition with retrograde Saturn, forming a Grand Cross on 29 May, with Jupiter and the Moon's North Node also in opposition to Neptune. The integrated physical, emotional and spiritual levels of the heart are challenging the final remnants of old beliefs, ideals and spiritual structures that inhibit the expression of the new heart-centred spirituality that is taking root. At the same time, the spiritual vision for the future is demanding the full release of the old Piscean archetypes, particularly those concerned with all forms of spiritual elitism. What matters now is the state of each individual's heart.

The Grand Cross begins to weaken on 7 June, as the Sun and Venus move on, but it continues (with Mercury and Vesta) until 23 June.

More Grand Trines and Kites

On 3 July a Water Grand Trine forms between Venus (in Cancer), Mars (in Scorpio) and retrograde Chiron (in Pisces). This represents another positive stage in the emotional healing process between the feminine and the masculine. Retrograde Chiron, in the last degrees of Pisces, brings to the surface more patterns from the Age of Pisces that still need to be healed, while Venus is deepening the inner marriage of the opposites. Mars is speaking its truth, to make others aware of what needs to be healed, particularly in our relationship with the Earth.

By 10 July, Venus is joined by Mercury and the Sun, making this healing process ever more conscious; this GT dissolves after 24 July. Meanwhile, a Kite will have been formed, on 22 July, by all four of the asteroids. Ceres, at the head of the Kite (in Taurus), leads the way forward, bringing the integrated energies of the human soul to renew and re-energize the Earth. Ceres is supported in this by Vesta (in Gemini) integrating the heart and mind, by Juno (in Scorpio) releasing the old emotional attachments of the ego, and by Pallas (in Pisces) bringing the clarity of mind to release us from the limiting spiritual beliefs of the Piscean Age.

On 30 July, a second Kite forms with Mercury at the head, again supported by Vesta (now in Cancer), Juno and Pallas. This will bring to the rational mind an understanding of what was emerging from the other Kite, at the soul level. On 6 August, Mercury is replaced by Venus, enabling integration of these balanced soul energies at the conscious emotional level of the personality; then both Kites dissolve on 11 August.

On 15 August, *another* Grand Trine forms between Vesta (in Cancer), Juno (in Scorpio) and retrograde Neptune (in Pisces). Neptune is continuing the dissolution of old Piscean attachments and archetypes, freeing us to be able to relate fully from the heart.

On 27 August, this GT becomes a Kite, as the Sun and Moon's North Node move into position at its head. On 4 September, just as the Kite dissolves, Sun and Node become exactly conjunct; this is the moment when the conscious ego, aligned with the inner heart, can fully grasp its spiritual purpose, and understand how to become free from the illusions and attachments of the past, and from perceived separation, by surrendering to the all-embracing Unconditional Love of the Universe.

Such a profound realization will take some time to integrate at the personality level. This will be helped by the conjunction of Mars and Pluto on 19 October, forming a 'Learning Triangle' with the Moon's North Node and the Moon. The masculine energy of the personal and spiritual will become completely aligned, so that our spiritual purpose can be understood and integrated at the emotional level.

This realization will be further enhanced as Venus becomes exactly conjunct with Saturn on 30 October. This brings integration at emotional and physical levels, and understanding of how to align the personal and spiritual will with our life's purpose. Venus then moves on to become conjunct Pluto on 25 November. This again reinforces the process of integration between the personal masculine will (Mars), and the personal feminine feelings (Venus), with our overall spiritual will (Pluto) and soul's purpose (Moon's Node).

December Solstice 2016

The long process of transformation and rebirth, which began way back at the December Solstice in 1999, moves toward completion at the December Solstice 2016. Ceres will move direct on 10 December, and Uranus will move direct on 30 December, either side of the Solstice on 21 December.

Ceres and Uranus will have been in conjunction since the beginning of June 2016, becoming exact on 23 June and 10 December.

As the Solstice Sun emerges, reborn from the Dark Rift of the Galactic Centre for the last time, this conjunction brings the alignment of Heaven (Uranus) and Earth (Ceres), following the four-year process of integration between the feminine and masculine aspects of consciousness, since the December Solstice of 2012.

Conclusion

Collectively, we will be poised and ready to move forward into the 'Fifth Sun' cycle of the balanced expression of the feminine and masculine; integrating this within our individual human consciousness; expressing this integration in the world through our diverse societies and cultures, through our political and economic structures, and through all of our interrelations.

There will also be a balance between the energies of Spirit and the energies of Earth. This will reflect our preparedness to move forward and manifest the energetic frequencies of 'As Above, so Below', depicted by the zodiac symbol of Aquarius – ♒ – as we move into the Age of Aquarius.

As the 2016 December Solstice Sun emerges from the depths of the Mayans' *Xibalba-be*, the 'Road to the Underworld', we will be fully reborn from the Cosmic womb of Creation, and prepared for the next stage in our evolution, as it unfolds in the coming 5,125 years.

This is just the beginning of the new cycle. It will serve us well to remember that we are mere infants in terms of understanding and mastering the new levels of consciousness. One thing will be certain – the old ways, patterns, archetypes and paradigms from the Age of Pisces will have finally passed; we can no longer return to them or try to rekindle them, just as surely as we cannot return to the womb, once we have been reborn.

Now it is up to each person to choose to live fully from the heart; in so doing, we can bring to Earth the unlimited creative potentials carried by the Divine Wisdom, Spiritual Power and Unconditional Love that emanate from the Source of Creation, flowing through the Heart of the Galaxy toward us... the rest is up to us.

The End... and the Beginning

Appendix A
PRECESSION TIMELINE
SINCE 13,830 BCE

This timeline is based on the dates when the Northern Hemisphere Spring Equinox point (intersection of the Celestial Equator and Ecliptic) passes in front of the first stars of each zodiac constellation.

Previous Ages	Approx. Size of Constellation	Approx. Duration
Virgo	45°	13,830–10,600 BCE

The Golden Age

Referred to in Greek and Roman Mythology as the time when gods and goddesses walked on the Earth. The North Pole pointed toward Vega, brightest of all the Pole stars, in the constellation Lyra. Vega is associated with the Egyptian goddess Maat, the Spirit of Order. In Babylonian times, Vega was known as Dilgan, the 'Messenger of Light'; the Chinese included it in the constellation *Chih Neu*, the Spinning Damsel or Weaving Sister, her qualities similar to Virgo. Toward the end of the Golden Age of Virgo, the midwinter Sun began its 13,000-year journey through the 'Galactic Winter'.

Previous Ages	Approx. Size of Constellation	Approx. Duration
Leo	37°	10,600–7900 BCE

Age of the Lion

Possible origins of the Sphinx[1] and the worship of Sekhmet, the Lion Goddess, are associated with this age. As a Fire Age, this brought about increasing global temperatures, resulting in the melting of the polar Ice Caps at the end of the last Ice Age. Toward the end of this age, this resulted in the Great Flood, referred to in the Bible and in Plato's account of the sinking of Atlantis.

• •

Cancer	20°	7900–6500 BCE

Age of the Goddess

The establishment of permanent towns and cities dominated the age. Cancer is concerned with hearth and home, family and tribe. This age brought the ascendancy of the Goddess and the creation of the first city-states. With the development of agriculture and permanent settlements, this enabled tribal cultures to extend and create larger social structures.

• •

Gemini	27°	6500–4490 BCE

Age of the Twins

Age of the Twins infers communication between Heaven and Earth. The Age of the Divine Twins was probably the time when the myth of Osiris and Isis originated. Osiris and Isis were both brother and sister, and husband and wife, representing the balanced male and female aspects of the Divine. This was the Age of Thoth-Hermes, the great lawgiver of the spiritual mysteries, who brought the gift of writing to mankind.

Previous Ages	Approx. Size of Constellation	Approx. Duration
Taurus	**40°**	**4490–1700 BCE**

Age of the Bull

This age brought bull-cults, bull-worship and the understanding and harnessing of Earth energies. It also brought the emergence of cultures that built powerful, globally interconnected structures, such as the Pyramids, Stonehenge, standing stones and stone circles. Spirituality was based on understanding and working with the rhythms and relationships between the Earth, Moon, Sun and stars.

• •

Aries	**23°**	**1700–6 BCE**

Age of Heroes

This was the age of the heroic journey, and development of belief systems about a single, all-powerful Deity. The emergence of monotheistic religions, such as Judaism and Zoroastrianism, brought strong, heroic and powerful prophets, leaders and warriors (eg: Abraham, Moses, Jason), who undertook spiritually challenging journeys and quests.

• •

Pisces	**38°**	**CE 6–2600**

Age of Mysticism, Monotheism, Global Religions and Global Relations

The fishes swimming in opposite directions symbolize the pull to explore both the spiritual realms and physical realms, which were perceived as opposites. This Age was concerned with understanding the relationship between this apparent duality and learning how to integrate these two levels of consciousness. Because of the length of Pisces (38°), there is an extended period of transition between the Ages of Pisces and Aquarius.

Previous Ages	Approx. Size of Constellation	Approx. Duration
Aquarius	**25°**	CE **2600–4600**

Age of Balancing Individual and Group Consciousness

Aquarius, the Water Bearer, represents the 'coming of age' of Humanity, when we will understand our true spiritual nature and responsibility to one another and to the Earth. As we extend our horizons out into Space, this needs to be balanced by also extending our inner psychological and spiritual horizons, enabling us to understand our place within the Cosmos and our spiritual responsibilities toward It.

APPENDIX B
PLANETS AND ZODIAC SIGN SYMBOLS

The Planets

Symbol		Key Words
☉	Sun	Sense of self, identity, centre, heart-mind, father
☽	Moon	Feeling self, emotional self, inner child
☿	Mercury	Thinking, communication, rational mind
♀	Venus	Relationships, beauty, femininity, sexual/emotional attraction, artistic creativity
♂	Mars	Drive, will, activity, focus, masculinity, sexual/emotional desire
⚳	Ceres	Physical nourishment, spiritual nurture, spiritual connection with the Earth
⚴	Pallas Athene	Intuitive intelligence, female warrior, self-protection, emotional boundaries
⚶	Vesta	Spiritual heart, essence, kundalini, hearth and home, inner peace

Symbol		Key Words
⚹	Juno	Karmic relationship patterns, soul relationship, soul contracts
♃	Jupiter	Creative mind, imagination, vision, purpose, inner and outer journeying
♄	Saturn	Physical self, limitations, fears, mother, boundaries, responsibility, Shadow
⚷	Chiron	Wounded healer, shaman, magician, maverick, spiritual creativity
♅	Uranus	Spiritual intuition, wisdom, insight, radical change, awakening
♆	Neptune	Spiritual inspiration, Unconditional Love, compassion, seeing through illusion and delusion
♇	Pluto	Spiritual will, power, transformation, pure light of be-ing
☊	Moon's North Node	Future purpose, spiritual growth, possibilities for spiritual fulfilment
☋	Moon's South Node	Past life patterns, ancestry, karma, release from the past

The Zodiac Signs

Symbol	Element	Key Words for 2012
♈ Aries	*Fire*	Self-control, cultivating equanimity of heart and spiritual poise
♉ Taurus	*Earth*	Release past attachments, discover service to the Earth, manifest spiritual beauty
♊ Gemini	*Air*	Connect mind and heart, find mental constancy, emotional commitment, and still point
♋ Cancer	*Water*	Be aware of emotional effect on the whole of Humanity, as family, and on the Earth
♌ Leo	*Fire*	Selfless creativity, find true spiritual family, cultivate emotional independence
♍ Virgo	*Earth*	See the perfection inherent in everything now, use spiritual discernment and integrity
♎ Libra	*Air*	Connect with Earth, include personal needs, transcend limiting belief systems
♏ Scorpio	*Water*	Confront emotional Shadow, release grief, embrace cycles of birth, growth, decay, and renewal

Symbol		Element	Key Words for 2012
♐	Sagittarius	*Fire*	Find inner stillness, trust intuition, live in the moment, remain grounded
♑	Capricorn	*Earth*	Create emotional support, delegate power, embrace vulnerability, surrender
♒	Aquarius	*Air*	Let go of rigid thinking, embrace uncertainty, balance individual and group
♓	Pisces	*Water*	Create strong boundaries and clear individuality, to express compassion and Unconditional Love

CHAPTER NOTES

Introduction

1. The Mayan civilization is believed to have developed around 2000 BCE, gradually spreading throughout the region of Central America that we know today as Guatemala, Honduras, El Salvador, Yucatan and Central Mexico.
2. The 'Age of Enlightenment', which emerged during the 18th century in Europe and North America, focused on reason and science as the accepted means for understanding and verifying how the natural world works.

Chapter 1

1. Richard Tarnas, *Cosmos and Psyche*, p. 50.
2. The New Testament *Matthew 9:14-17, Mark 2:18-22,* and *Luke 5:33-39.*

Chapter 2

1. John Major Jenkins, *Maya Cosmogenesis 2012*, pp. 229–230.
2. According to J. Kelly Beatty, Senior Contributing Editor of *Sky & Telescope*.
3. The 'Archetypes of the Unconscious' were defined and explored in great detail by the renowned psychologist, Carl Gustav Jung (1875–1961), the founder of Analytical Psychology. Archetypes are universal psychological 'forms',

which can be found in different cultures throughout the world, for example, the Wise Man, the Wise Woman, the Hero, the Trickster, the Great Mother, and so on.

4. Giorgio de Santillana & Hertha von Dechend, *Hamlet's Mill*.

5. Gary Renard, *The Disappearance of the Universe* p. 183.

6. K.E. Maltwood, *A Guide to Glastonbury's Temple of the Stars*.

7. Joseph Campbell, *The Masks of God, vol II: Oriental Mythology* p. 14.

Chapter 3

1. The psychological Shadow was described by the psychologist Carl Gustav Jung as one of the principal archetypes of the Unconscious: 'Unfortunately there can be no doubt that man is, on the whole, less good than he imagines himself or wants to be. Everyone carries a shadow, and the less it is embodied in the individual's conscious life, the blacker and denser it is. If an inferiority is conscious, one always has a chance to correct it. Furthermore, it is constantly in contact with other interests, so that it is continually subjected to modifications. But if it is repressed and isolated from consciousness, it never gets corrected.'
C.G. Jung *Collected Works: Psychology and Religion: West and East* (1938), p. 131.

Chapter 4

1. Nigel Twinn, *Hamish Miller, a Life Divined*, pp. 87–88. Hamish Miller (1927–2010) was a renowned dowser who, with Paul Broadhurst, in the 1980s dowsed the length of the now famous 'Michael–Mary' energy line running across Southern England. In the 1990s they followed the 'Apollo–Athene' line from Ireland, through Europe to Israel. The fascinating story of these remarkable spiritual journeys is

described in *The Sun and the Serpent* and *The Dance of the Dragon.*

2. The North–South Meridians (or MC lines) of the planets are shown on the Eclipse Map as solid vertical lines passing through the circular planetary 'glyphs' on the map. The circular glyphs mark the exact position of the planet, directly overhead at that moment.

3. Robert Coon, *Earth Chakras,* p. 247.

4. For a further exploration about the true significance of the Holy Grail, see Rudolf Steiner's lecture on The Gospel of St John - VII: The Mystery of Golgotha, available at www.rsarchive.org/Lectures; see also the ideas explored in *The Holy Blood and the Holy Grail* by Michael Baigent, Richard Leigh & Henry Lincoln.

5. Paul Broadhurst and Hamish Miller, with Vivienne Shanley and Ba Russell, *The Dance of the Dragon.*

6. Robert Bauval and Adrian Gilbert, *The Orion Mystery.*

7. Alice A Bailey, *A Treatise on the Seven Rays.*

8. Richard Hinckley Allen, *Star Names*, p. 298.

9. Bernadette Brady, *Brady's Book of Fixed Stars*, p. 105.

10. Hesiod (translated by A.N. Athanassakis), *Works and Days,* verses 14–24.

Chapter 5

1. This process of alignment between the Galactic Centre and the Earth's Core is beautifully and clearly described by Barbara Hand Clow in *Alchemy of Nine Dimensions*, Part I, Chapter 1.

2. See the inspiring energy grid work of William Buehler at www.shameer-orion.org. For a PDF of Hawaii Roil point go to Index of PDF, then click, RoilPointTemplaMar01.pdf.

3. Richard Tarnas, *Cosmos and Psyche*, p. 307 et seq.

4. Richard Tarnas, *Cosmos and Psyche*, pp. 300–302.

Chapter 6

1. The story of this is told in *The Greenpeace Story* by Michael Brown and John May.
2. D. Freidel, L. Schele & J. Parker, *Maya Cosmos*, p. 96.
3. John Major Jenkins, *Maya Cosmogenesis 2012*, pp. 81–85.

Chapter 7

1. *The Sabian Symbols in Astrology* by Dr Marc Edmund Jones describes 360 symbolic images, one for each degree of the zodiac. They were clairvoyantly received in 1925 by Miss Elsie Wheeler in San Diego, then transcribed and interpreted by astrologer Dr Marc Edmund Jones. They offer profound insights into the spiritual qualities behind a planet's position in a particular degree; sometimes their meaning is obscure and, at others, startlingly clear.

   The Sabian Symbols were later reinterpreted by Dane Rudhyar, in *An Astrological Mandala*, which gives more modern (and sometimes more easily comprehensible) interpretations.
2. Dane Rudhyar, *An Astrological Mandala* (Random House, Inc.) p. 61.

Chapter 8

1. D. Freidel, L. Schele & J. Parker, *Maya Cosmos*, p. 53.

Chapter 9

1. See various translations of *Dao de Jing*, Chap 29.

Appendix A

1. See Graham Hancock & Robert Bauval, *The Message of the Sphinx;* also, Robert M. Schoch's research, www.robertschoch.com.

BIBLIOGRAPHY

Allan, D. D. & Delair, J. B., *Cataclysm!*, Bear & Co

Allen, R. H., *Star Names*, Dover Publications

Arroyo, Stephen, *Astrology, Karma and Transformation*, CRCS Publications

Baigent, Michael, Leigh, Richard & Lincoln, Henry, *The Holy Blood and the Holy Grail*, Corgi Books

Bailey, Alice A., *Treatise on the Seven Rays*, Lucis Trust

Bauval, Robert & Gilbert, Adrian, *The Orion Mystery*, Crown Trade Paperbacks

Brady, Bernadette, *Brady's Book of Fixed Stars*, Red Wheel/Weiser

Brailsford, Barry, *The Chronicles of the Stone*, Stoneprint Press

Broadhurst, Paul & Miller, Hamish, *The Dance of the Dragon*, Pendragon Press

Broadhurst, Paul & Miller, Hamish, *The Sun and the Serpent*, Pendragon Press

Brown, Michael & May, John, *The Greenpeace Story*, Dorling Kindersley, Inc.

Calasso, Roberto, *The Marriage of Cadmus and Harmony*, Vintage

Joseph Campbell, *The Masks of God, vol II: Oriental Mythology*, Penguin Arkana

Campbell, Joseph, *Occidental Mythology: The Masks of God*, Penguin/Compass

Case, Paul Foster, *The Tarot*, Macoy Publishing

Castledine, David B. (translator), *Popol Vuh*, Monclem Ediciones

Clow, Barbara Hand, *Alchemy of Nine Dimensions*, Hampton Roads

Clow, Barbara Hand, *Catastrophobia*, Bear & Co.

Coon, Robert, *Earth Chakras*, Robert Coon

de Troyes, Cretien, translated by Nigel Bryant, *Perceval – The Story of the Grail*, D.S. Brewer

Friedel, David, Schele, Linda & Parker, Joy, *Maya Cosmos*, Perennial/HarperCollins

George, Andrew (translation), *The Epic of Gilgamesh*, Penguin Classics

George, Demetra with Douglas Bloch, *Asteroid Goddesses*, ACS Publications

Graves, Robert, *The Greek Myths*, Penguin Books

Greene, Liz, *Relating*, Thorsons

Greene, Liz, *Saturn:a new look at an old devil*, The Aquarian Press

Greene, Liz, *The Astrological Neptune, and the Quest for Redemption*, Weiser Books,

Hancock, Graham & Bauval, Robert, *The Message of the Sphinx*, Crown Publishers

Hesiod (Translation by A. N. Athanassakis), *Theogony, Works and Days, Shield*, Johns Hopkins

Jenkins, John Major, *Maya Cosmogenesis 2012*, Bear & Co

Jones, Dr Marc Edmund, *The Sabian Symbols in Astrology*, Aurora Press

Jung, Carl Gustav, Jung, Emma & von Franz, Marie-Louise, *Collected Works: The Grail Legend*, Princeton University Press

Lao-Tzu, *Dao de Jing* (various translations)

Maltwood, K. E., *A Guide to Glastonbury's Temple of the Stars*, James Clarke & Co.

Morse, Dr Eric, *The Living Stars*, Amethyst Books

Myss, Caroline, *Sacred Contracts*, Bantam Books

Oken, Alan, *Soul-Centred Astrology*, Crossing Press

Pila of Hawaii, *The Secrets and Mysteries of Hawaii*, Health Communications

Pollack, Rachel, *Seventy-Eight Degrees of Wisdom*, The Aquarian Press

Renard, Gary R., *The Disappearance of the Universe*, Hay House

Ray, Sondra, *Pele's Wish*, New World Library

Rudhyar Dane, *An Astrological Mandala*, Random House, Inc.

de Santillana, Giorgio & von Dechend, Hertha *Hamlet's Mill*, Godine

Scott, Mary, *Kundalini in the Physical World*, Arkana

Schulman, Martin, *Karmic Astrology: The Moon's Nodes and Reincarnation*, The Aquarian Press

Settegast, Mary, *Plato Prehistorian*, Lindisfarne Press

Tarnas, Richard, *Cosmos and Psyche*, Plume

Twinn, Nigel, *Hamish Miller: A Life Divined*, Penwith Press

Tyler, Pamela H., *Mercury*, Aquarian Press

Ulansey, David, *The Origins of the Mithraic Mysteries*, Oxford University Press

Vidler, Mark, *The Star Mirror*, Thorsons HarperCollins